Essential Guide
to
Multifunction
Optical Storage

Essential Guide to Multifunction Optical Storage

Edited by Judith Paris Roth

Meckler

Westport ▪ London

Library of Congress Cataloging-in-Publication Data

Essential guide to multifunction optical storage / edited by Judith
    Paris Roth.
        p.   cm.
    Includes bibliographical references and index.
    ISBN 0-88736-751-8 : $
    1. Optical storage devices. 2. Data disk drives. I. Roth,
Judith Paris. II. Title: Multifunction optical storage.
TK7895.M4E78   1991
621.39'767–dc20   91-35068
                                                                CIP

British Library Cataloguing-in-Publication Data is available.

Meckler Publishing, the publishing division of Meckler Corporation,
    11 Ferry Lane West, Westport, CT 06880.
Meckler Ltd., 247-249 Vauxhall Bridge Road, London SW1V 1HQ, U.K.

Printed on acid free paper.
Printed and bound in the United States of America.

For Bryan, Rachel Annaliese, and Our Future

Contents

List of Trademarks

Trademark	Company
Unix	AT&T Bell Laboratories
Macintosh	Apple Computers
VAX/VMS, Unibus, Q-bus	Digital Equipment Corporation (DEC)
HP-UX	Hewlett-Packard Company
MCA,PS/2,OS/2	IBM Corporation
Xenix, MS-DOS, PC-DOS	Microsoft Corporation
NeXTStep, Mach	NeXT, Inc.
ETOM	Optex Corporation
LaserVision	Sony Corporation of America
Sun, SunOS	Sun Microsystems
THOR-CD	Tandy Corporation

Introduction

I ntroduced in 1990 after years of intensive research and development efforts throughout the world, multifunction (an integrated WORM [write-once, read-many]/rewritable disk drive) optical storage offers the computer and communications industry a viable, durable, reliable online mass storage device for workstations, "plug-and-play" subsystems, PCs, and mini- and mainframe computers. The write-once (W-O) and rewritable characteristics of a multifunction optical disk drive (sometimes referred to as hybrid or dual-function drives) allow the end-user and systems integrator to use the technology as both primary and secondary mass storage with standalone and multi-user networks offering advantages over magnetic storage for historical archival storage, unattended back/up/restore storage, and document storage and retrieval methods. Multifunction optical storage, as described by Hewlett-Packard (H-P), "provides flexibility to grow applications from single functionality to multifunctionality."

The cost of a multifunction optical disk drive, while in the $5,000 range as compared with a $1,000 Winchester hard disk drive, offers a value-added dimension currently unavailable with Winchester drives; a multifunction optical disk drive offers the opportunity for both archival storage (using the W-O mode) as well as write/erase/rewrite capabilities in the rewritable mode.

Characteristics and Features of Multifunction Optical Storage

To better appreciate the unique characteristics and features of both WORM and rewritable optical disk technology, a correlation can be made with perceived benefits that result from these features in the following table.

Comparison of Write-once and Rewritable Optical Disk Storage Features and Benefits

Features	Benefits
Removability	Transportability Security
Cartridge	Add cartridges versus drives Reduced cost per megabyte Fewer mounts and dismounts
Erasable	Reusable media Lower cost per megabyte
High-storage capacity	Reduced storage space and costs Lower costs for additional megabytes
Jukebox capability	Online access to data Near-line access to large databases Unattended operation
Large online databases	Low waiting cost High usage Unattended operations Higher productivity
Random access	Faster access time (compared to tape) Increased response time
Data security	No head crashes Ten year data life with reusability
Data interchange	Transportable media with standards Allows data interchange between sites Compatible with existing equipment

This table is reprinted from *Rewritable Optical Storage Technology*, Edited by J.P. Roth, Meckler Corporation (Westport, CT), 1990.

Multifunction Optical Disk Drives: An Overview

A variety of Japanese manufacturers have announced their intention to manufacture multifunction or hybrid drives, and a number of them have already introduced products both in Japan and the United States: Pioneer, Hewlett-Packard, Sony, Nippon Telephone and Telegraph (NTT), and Kokusai Denshin Denwa Company, Ltd. (KDD). As early as 1988, NTT demonstrated an early prototype of a multifunction optical disk drive at an IEEE conference.

There are three essential approaches to multifunction optical storage:

1.   *Sampled Servo*, supported by Laser Magnetic Storage International (LMSI), Optical Storage Corporation (OSC), Optimem, Philips and Du Pont Optical (PDO), Pioneer, and TDK Electronics, locates servo-burst information between data sectors. Rewritable media is magneto-optical (M-O).

2.   *Direct-Overwrite*, supported primarily by Panasonic and Reflection Systems, uses a single pass (direct overwrite technology) because it employs phase-change (P-C) media rather than (M-O).

3.   *Continuous Composite* is supported by a consortium of over fourteen firms: 3M, Asahi, Daicel, Fuji, H-P, Kuraray, Maxoptix, Mitsui, Nixdorf, Olympus, OSC, PDO, Ricoh, Seiko Epson, and Sony. Formed in July 1990, this consortium is working to establish interchange format and media specification standards for multifunction optical disk drives.

At the spring 1990 COMDEX show, both Panasonic Communications and Systems Company and Pioneer Communications of America introduced multifunction optical disk drives. Pioneer has developed a multifunction optical drive, the DE-U7001, which offers both W-O and rewritable functions. Pioneer's drive was first introduced in Japan and is now available in the United States. Pioneer users will be able to select either temporary (rewritable) or permanent (WORM) storage. The DE-U7001 drive is capable of writing data to and reading data from both types of disks (W-O and rewritable) and its single drive switches modes through commands generated automatically by the host computer.

The Pioneer drive is being sold by LMSI, Optimem, OSC, Pioneer, and TDK. The DE-U7001 conforms to an International Organization for Standardization (ISO) draft for Sampled Servo (SS) format and has a 327MB storage capacity per disk side; it uses Pioneer's currently available WORM media. Pioneer, LMSI, and PDO are offering rewritable SS optical media for the Pioneer drive at about $200 per double-sided cartridge.

LMSI, Optimem, and Pioneer multifunction optical disk drives use an SS format developed by the ISO which allows rewritable and WORM media to be interchanged. At least four media manufacturers have agreed to produce both rewritable and WORM media in the SS format for the new drives: Daicel, PDO, Pioneer Video Company, and TDK, Ltd. Companies have disclosed plans to work together to ensure compatibility between their products.

H-P has released a multifunction optical disk drive, the HP C1716M, and has provided multifunction optical capabilities in its 20GB optical disk jukebox. Based on rewritable continuous composite M-O format, media is permanently identified as W-O or rewritable at the time of its manufacture. The H-P optical disk drive provides data security by identifying the media type and then invoking the appropriate command set. The W-O command set does not include commands that destroy data (erase or reformat); the rewritable command set allows unlimited writing and erasures.

Other optical firms that have announced multifunction drives include Ricoh, which has demonstrated a 5.25-inch "dual function" (write-once and rewritable) drive, the RO-5042, in Japan. It is expected that Maxtor will eventually market the Ricoh multifunction optical disk drive in the United States as part of a subsystem sometime in 1991.

Panasonic's 5.25-inch multifunction optical disk drive uses direct overwrite P-C technology. Thus, the LF-7010 does not conform to ISO/ANSI (American National Standards Institute) proposed standards for M-O technology. (See section on standards p. xiv-xv.) However, using P-C technology, direct overwrite can significantly increase write operations because it does not have to first erase a sector before rewriting. Reflection Systems, Inc. offers the RF-10J and RF-11JM desktop jukeboxes based on the Panasonic multifunction optical disk

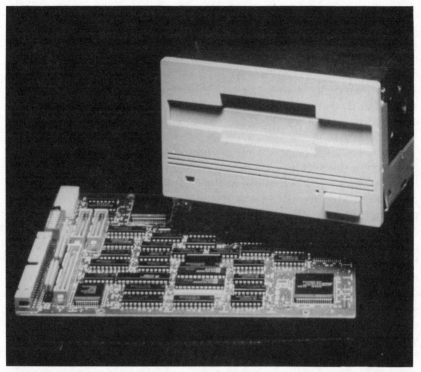

Figure 1. The HP C1716M Multifunction Optical Disk Drive. Courtesy Hewlett-Packard Company.

drive.

While P-C and W-O optical media are considered more compatible than M-O and W-O media for use in a multifunction drive, only Panasonic has officially introduced a multifunction product or plans for developing drives that include P-C media. Literal Corporation (Colorado Springs, CO) offers 5.25-inch multifunction optical drives using P-C optical media.

Multifunction optical disk drives are now being integrated in a growing number of "plug-and-play" subsystems available from VARs, system integrators, and other OEMs. Computer Upgrade Corporation, Ten X Technology, DynaTek Automation Systems, and other system integrators are developing multifunction optical disk products for MS-DOS, OS/2, NeXT, SCO Xenix, Unibus and Q-bus computers, VAX/VMS, Unix, Sun, and Macintosh environments.

Standards for Multifunction (WORM/Rewritable) Optical Storage

ANSI is working on two proposed national standards: CCS (Continuous Composite Servo) and SS for 5.25-inch (130mm) rewritable optical disks. ANSI has also begun work on developing a standard for rewritable 3.5-inch disks as well. Each of these formats accommodates both WORM and rewritable optical disks. Generally, all rewritable optical disk drives, except for the Canon M-O non-ISO standard drive, use the CCS format.

The ANSI 5.25-inch rewritable optical disk standards project is based on the 5.25-inch WORM CCS but there are a few differences to account for the M-O nature of the read-write process. The goal of the X3B11 committee is to allow a multifunction optical disk drive that could handle both WORM and rewritable CCS media.

The optical rewritable standard documents include a fairly extensive chapter on defect management which details how a scheme for defective sector retirement should be implemented (Berg and Roth, 1989).

Interchangeability is one of *the* key standards issues to resolve. Although standards will allow data interchange between different manufacturers' products, data interchange is still all but impossible between currently available units (Apiki and Eglowstein, 1989). In the fall of 1990, H-P announced its participation in developing a standard format for file interchange on WORM and rewritable optical disk drives. ANSI has accredited a twelve member committee, X3B11.1, to produce the standard.

Media interchangeability between ANSI/ISO compliant drives will allow customers to use any ANSI/ISO media rather than rely on a single proprietary media source. PDO, Sony, and 3M manufacture rewritable media that comply with ANSI/ISO standards which allow for media interchangeability.

Development of a multifunction optical disk drive (5.25 and 3.5 inch) will resolve the debate over using W-O or rewritable optical storage. Moreover, future generations of multifunction optical storage are sure to offer the end-user and system integrator a device that can read and write rewritable, WORM, and read-only optical storage.

As W-O, rewritable, and read-only optical technologies are merged into multifunction or hybrid optical disk drives, their competition among the formats will diminish. Backward compatibility, software tools, alternative and established media sources, data interchangeability standards, and transportability will continue to be critical challenges to the optical storage industry, especially for rewritable optical storage if it is to change the computer industry's current storage and retrieval practices.

Organization of this Book

This book provides accurate information about the basics of multifunction including rewritable optical storage technology and how it can be creatively used for information storage and retrieval. The book's chapters are written by people at companies actively pursuing development of multifunction optical storage, primarily drive and media manufacturers.

This book assumes the reader has a basic knowledge of optical storage. It is intended to provide an overview and comparison of the basic technological approaches to multifunction optical storage, media, and drive development; offer a look at the proposed standards, and the debate over continuous composite write-once (CCW) versus SS. It is based largely on articles published in the January/February 1991 issue of *Optical Information Systems*.

The terms "rewritable" and "erasable" are used interchangeably throughout this book. In addition, erasability refers to the ability to *intentionally* delete data sectors rather than accidental erasure or editing.

The *Essential Guide to Multifunction Optical Storage* is divided into the following six chapters:

Chapter 1. *Developing and Choosing Multifunctional Optical Storage: Problems and Solutions*. Written by a major developer of Sony's rewritable optical storage technology, this chapter examines the history of multifunction's introduction. The history of information systems is analogous to the history of the television industry. First there were books, then radio and television. Information systems in the data storage area started with the letter, then audio/video and ROM. W-O was developed using such media as typewriters, microfilm, and 8mm movie film to store information. Society is continually looking for more capability for information storage that is rewritable such as FDD, MOD, and VCR. Moreover, these capabilities should be easily accessible. Optical storage technology has followed this same type of pattern starting with LD, CD, CD-ROM, W-O and then rewritable (M-O). Customers now want all of these capabilities in a single drive represented by the multifunction optical disk drive.

Chapter 2. *Continuous Composite Multifunction Optical Storage*. A new multifunction optical disk technology based on the ISO Continuous Composite (CC) recording format has been developed by Hewlett-Packard Company. This new format provides the flexibility of rewritable and the permanency of write-once optical storage. Media and drive identifiers distinguish between the two media types and permit both to meet their application requirements in one multifunction optical disk drive. This chapter discusses H-P's approach to using CC optical storage and proposed draft standards for Continuous Composite Write-Once Media.

Chapter 3. *Using Phase-Change Technology with Direct Overwrite in a Multifunction Optical Disk Drive.* In June 1990, at the COMDEX Spring trade show, Panasonic (Matsushita Electric Industrial, Ltd. Co.) introduced the world's first P-C with a direct overwrite multifunction (WORM/rewritable) optical disk drive. This chapter describes the background and reasoning behind using P-C technology with direct overwrite and compares it with two competing multifunction approaches. In addition, the author discusses the trade-offs among the alternative technologies.

Chapter 4. *Answering the Need for WORM and Rewritable Optical Storage: The Multifunction Optical Disk Drive.* In July 1990, Pioneer Communications of America became the first company to develop, market, and ship a multifunction rewritable/WORM optical disk drive. Seven other companies have announced their intention to develop and sell compatible drives and media for the 5.25-inch ISO SS format device including LMSI, Optimem, OSC, PDO, and TDK. This chapter describes the development of the multifunction optical disk drive, its technical specifications, features, advantages, benefits, and applications in the developing market. It focuses on how the system works and why Pioneer chose to base its system on the SS format.

Chapter 5. *Rewritable Media Manufacturing for Multifunctional Drives.* With the coming of W-O and rewritable optical media, data storage in government, education, business, and industry is being transformed. As this transition from magnetic to optical storage has developed worldwide, the question has become: How can we achieve the permanence of W-O media and the flexibility of rewritable media all with one optical disk drive? PDO supports ISO standard formats of multifunction optical disk drives. A brief overview of quality rewritable media production in the world of multifunctionality is provided from the media manufacturer's perspective.

Chapter 6. *Software Considerations for Rewritable and Multifunction Optical Disk Drives.* Originally published in Issue 10:6 (November/December, 1990) of *Optical Information Systems* magazine, this chapter discusses basic file management software considerations germane to rewritable and multifunction optical disk drives. Written by a well-known optical storage software authority, this chapter includes a brief comparison of software for write-once with rewritable optical media. Implications of different rewritable optical media formats (P-C and M-O) for system and drive performance are discussed.

A technical glossary of terms and acronyms, a directory of companies working with multifunction and rewritable optical storage as well as a list of recommended readings are provided at the end of the book.

Mention of any company, product or service does not imply endorsement. Discussion of a product or company does not imply its superiority over competing applications, products, or systems. The errors, inaccuracies, and misstatements contained in this book are the authors'.

It is difficult, if not impossible, to publish a book about a dynamic technology, especially when technological breakthroughs, new product announcements and applications are the rule rather than the exception. This book is intended to help the reader become aware of the strengths and limitations of multifunction optical storage, and provide a knowledge base to help make information decisions about its development and use in our information society. Readers should consider this volume the beginning of an ongoing educational and evaluative process concerning optical storage technology, markets and application developments.

As of the writing of this introduction (spring, 1991), IBM was preparing its rewritable optical disk drives for market introduction. At that time, IBM had made no formal (or informal) announcement of its intention to develop and market a multifunction optical disk subsystem. However, given its involvement with rewritable and WORM optical storage, it is expected that IBM will eventually offer multifunction optical storage.

Chapter One

Developing and Choosing Multifunctional Optical Storage: Problems and Solutions

Takeshi Yazawa

I n 1970 Sony's expertise in numerous technical fields enabled the company to begin spearheading the development of optical disk recording technology. In the late 1970s Sony developed a high-performance semi-conductor laser as well as advanced optical pickup devices which led to the LaserVision disc, the interactive videodisc.

In 1982 Sony played a key role in ushering in the era of consumer digital audio technology with the world's first digital audio compact disc (CD). Based on the company's experience with CD technology, it offered a CD-ROM system in 1984, and in 1985 introduced Write-Once, Read-Many (WORM) optical disk drives and media.

Since the mid-1970s Sony has also been working on the research and development of terbium/iron/cobalt-based recording media allowing users to rewrite information numerous times while assuring the integrity of stored data. In 1983 Sony began joint development of 300mm rewritable optical disk products with Japan's International Telephone. Samples of 5.25-inch rewritable optical disk media and drives were shipped in the fall of 1987.

In October 1988, Sony became the first manufacturer to offer commercial rewritable optical disk drives and media. After this long-

1

awaited introduction of 5.25-inch rewritable optical technology, the optical business grew rapidly (before the end of 1989 over fifty rewritable optical-based systems were announced in the United States alone). This growth appears larger in rewritable than in any other optical product including ROM and write-once (W-O).

Sony's effort has contributed to the development of the rewritable optical business with the following support system (see Figure 1).

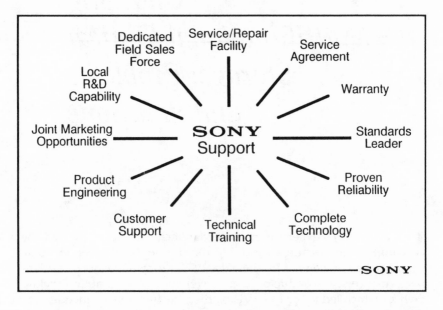

Figure 1. Sony Corporation Support Systems. Courtesy Sony Corporation of America.

Sony is now in a position between first-generation and second-generation optical products which will make the optical storage/re-cording market more popular with both the computer/communications industry and with a diverse array of end-users.

An analysis of the 5.25-inch rewritable optical market of the first generation, described in Figure 2, provides many answers in terms of price, specifications, usage and future demand. The charts in Figures 3 and 4 indicate data on rewritable optical industries and applications.

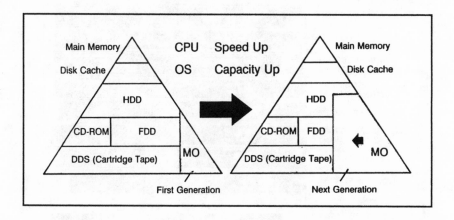

Figure 2. Data Storage Pyramid for WS.PC. Courtesy Sony Corporation of America.

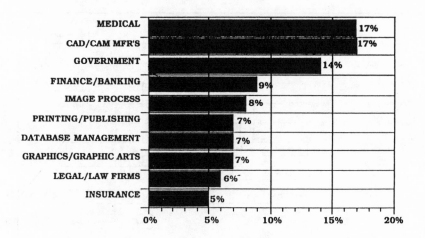

Figure 3. Industries Most Likely to Benefit From Rewritable Optical Technology. Courtesy Sony Corporation of America.

The data in these figures help to explain what Sony and other companies have to consider in order to expand the optical storage business. The technical growth path shown in Figure 5 can be expected as product development continues to search for higher specifications for access time, capacity, and transfer rates to incorporate into the next generation of rewritable optical products.

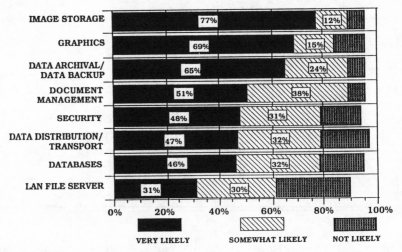

Figure 4. Applications Most Likely to Benefit from Rewritable Optical Products. Courtesy Sony Corporation of America.

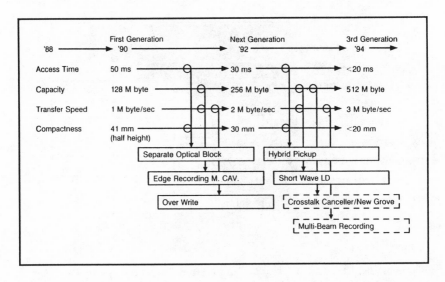

Figure 5. Technical Growth Path for 3.5-inch Rewritable Optical Disk. Courtesy Sony Corporation of America.

The above development activity is now advancing in R&D departments at many companies in the optical data storage industry. Rather than explain each of these technical developments today, the next section will focus on another subject——multifunction optical storage.

Let's consider the future direction using Figures 6 and 7. According to general market requirements, products always need to become more compact in size with more features such as multifunction.

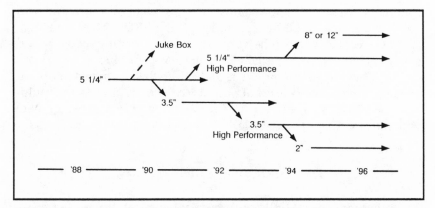

Figure 6. Future Direction (Disk Size). Courtesy Sony Corporation of America.

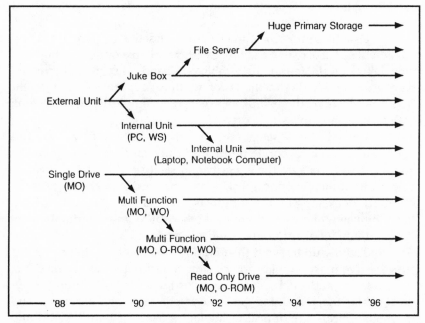

Figure 7. Future Direction (System Configuration). Courtesy Sony Corporation of America.

Considering all of the above information, Sony Corporation has found that one of the important capabilities is the multifunctional feature in order to maintain the current first generation of 5.25-inch rewritable optical products.

Medical, CAD/CAM, government, and finance industries continue to need W-O applications. Image storage, graphics, and data archival also need WORM capabilities. Optical-ROM Magneto-Optical (M-O) format will also be very important as multifunction optical storage is introduced, especially in 3.5-inch M-O products.

There are many products and future developments in optical storage. One of the futures of optical technical belongs to the multifunction optical disk drive which combines the permanence of W-O with the flexibility of rewritable.

The State of Optical Storage Today[1]

Taken individually, WORM and rewritable optical drives offer effective information management solutions for mass storage. However, combining the two technologies can be difficult due to their different purposes and methods.

Data files on WORM media are intended to be permanent and unalterable. This creates a conflict with rewritable optical technology which stresses stable but changeable data, and reusability of media. Also, existing WORM methods for writing data are vastly different from rewritable methods thus increasing the complexity of combining both technologies in a single drive.

With the right safeguards and the right technology, WORM applications can incorporate multi-level safeguards in both the media and the drive to ensure the integrity and safety of data. In all regards, Sony's multifunction optical disk drives and media meet or exceed the standards of existing WORM products but offer one significant advantage: by using one technology for both WORM and rewritable functions, multifunctionality is more reliably achieved.

To fully understand this solution, it is necessary to briefly discuss the five most popular optical storage techniques today. The first two, ablative and bubble-forming recording, are WORM-only solutions while the remaining three—dye-polymer, phase-change, and magneto-optical—are optical technologies used for both WORM and rewritable optical applications.

Ablative Recording

Ablative recording is a WORM technology that uses a laser to permanently alter media when writing data. To write, the laser focuses on the disk's metal recording layer with enough heat to create a hole, or "pit," in the recording surface. Once written, data cannot be easily altered or destroyed on ablative media. Behind the recording surface is a thin layer of air ("air sandwich") which is vented to the atmosphere to accommodate the expansion and vaporization of metal film during recording. The use of an air sandwich is unique to ablative media and a central part of its ability to record data.

To read, the ablative optical drive scans the disk and detects the pits that reflect differently than non-pitted areas. The drawback of ablative recording is the possible corrosion of media due to the air sandwich which exposes the disk's metal recording surface to the atmosphere.

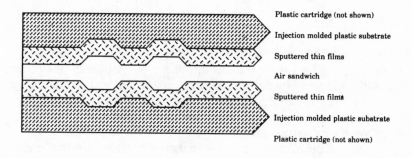

Figure 8. Ablative Media. Courtesy Hewlett-Packard Company.

Bubble-Forming Recording

Bubble-forming media consists of at least two recording layers in its substrate: a dielectric sublayer and a sputtered overlayer of heat-absorbing material. To write, the laser beam focuses through the dielectric sublayer and into the heat absorbing overlayer. The overlayer collects the heat and vaporizes the adjacent dielectric sublayer causing a subsurface bubble that deforms the heat-absorbing layer. The bubble changes the reflectivity of the data surface, a condition which is detected by the drive during reads. With effort, data on bubble forming media can be erased or altered although safeguards exist to prevent this from happening.

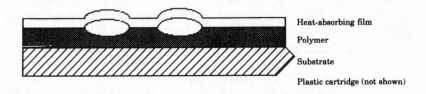

Figure 9. Bubble-Forming Recording. Courtesy Hewlett-Packard Company.

Dye-Polymer Recording

Dye-polymer (D-P) recording is a rewritable optical technology that can be adapted for use in WORM applications. A translucent plastic disk with a colored layer absorbs heat from the drive's laser beam and the heat creates a bump. Reading a D-P disk is similar to reading a bubble-forming disk; written areas are bumpy and reflect light differently than the unwritten areas.

While promising lower costs than the other rewritable technologies, the D-P solution is more complex. It requires two separate lasers each of a different wavelength making the drive more expensive. Moreover, the D-P media wears out after 1,000 to 10,000 write cycles.

Phase-Change Recording

Phase-change (P-C) recording is the second rewritable optical technology that can be adapted for use in WORM applications. Heat generated from the drive's laser changes the molecular structure of spots on the metal layer from an amorphous state to a crystalline state and back again. The amorphous and crystalline spots produce different levels of reflectivity, a condition which is detected by the drive during reads.

The problem with P-C recording rests with the drive which requires an expensive high-powered laser. Also, as with D-P methods, P-C media will not endure many rewrite cycles.

Magneto-Optical Recording

Magneto-optical (M-O) recording is the third technology that satisfies rewritable and WORM applications. Information on M-O media is stored in the form of magnetic flux directions rather than pits or bumps used in other optical technologies.

A major advantage is that M-O media can be written to and erased repeatedly with no measurable degradation of media or data. Conservative estimates of media life (based on accelerated lifewear testing) give M-O media a comparable, if not longer, life span than almost all existing optical media, making it extremely reliable for archival applications.

Magneto-optical Media

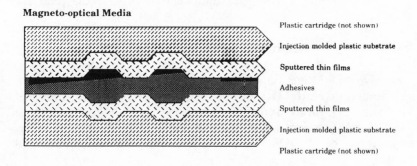

Plastic cartridge (not shown)

Injection molded plastic substrate

Sputtered thin films

Adhesives

Sputtered thin films

Injection molded plastic substrate

Plastic cartridge (not shown)

Figure 10. Magneto-Optical Recording. Courtesy Hewlett-Packard Company.

Can of WORMS

Whereas rewritable technologies offer benefits to archival applications, many companies still prefer WORM solutions. However, existing WORM technologies present certain market and technological limitations:

Problem: Most WORM drives are exclusive in purpose.
                  They perform well but are so specialized that

Problem:

they are capable of performing only one function.

Solution: Instead of specialized technologies, take advantage of a single standardized technology to address both W-O and rewritable needs.

Problem: Many WORM manufacturers use proprietary WORM method and media. As a result, standardization still exists as a barrier to the technology's acceptance in some areas. With a limited number of media suppliers, media prices have not decreased as they might have with the availability of multiple media sources.

Solution: Instead of using proprietary WORM media, use ISO/ANSI (International Organization for Standardization/American National Standards Institute) Continuous Composite Magneto-Optical media, and take advantage of existing standards and multiple media vendors.

Future State of Optical Storage

Currently, WORM is a popular archival solution but its methods appear limited given the lack of new WORM introductions in the last two years. The future of optical storage clearly rests in the development of multifunction drives and standardized media that combine the permanence of WORM with the flexibility of rewritable optical storage.

- *Multifunctionality.* WORM technology must not only coexist with rewritable technology, but also provide the option of using a single drive for both functions (media).
- *Standardization.* WORM drives and media should share the standards already in place for rewritable drives and media in order to leverage existing media sources and drive developments.
- *Reliability of data and media.* Long-term storage of valuable data must be reliable, stable and unquestioned.
- *Economies of scale.* WORM products should become more cost competitive as media and drive manufacturers proliferate.
- *Longevity of technology.* The WORM technology chosen today

should grow into the future and mirror the advancements made in rewritable technology.

Conclusion

With sophisticated protection measures in both the drive and media, archived data are safely and reliably stored indefinitely. Media can be obtained from many sources and the potential for standardization is very strong. The WORM/rewritable multifunction optical solution presents a logical approach to merging these functions in a single optical disk drive.

Chapter Two

Continuous Composite Multifunction Optical Storage

Christine Roby

W hen Hewlett-Packard Company (H-P) entered the optical storage market in the spring of 1989, many companies were concentrating their efforts on write-once, read-many (WORM) technologies. Why then did H-P begin with a rewritable optical disk drive and library system? The answers are market needs and standards.

H-P saw greater needs in the marketplace for rewritable optical storage. write-once (W-O) media can be written to only once and addresses applications that require as much permanency as technology will allow or are not subject to frequent revision. Rewritable optical, which allows virtually infinite write-erase-rewrite cycles, fills the storage gap between expensive online hard disk storage space and inexpensive but slow offline storage devices such as 1/2-inch tape. Rewritable optical technology provides direct access to large image and text files which would be prohibitively expensive to store on hard disks, but require frequent updating. When information is ready for backup or archive, rewritable optical technology is space efficient and, with removable media, easily secured or transported. These benefits have appeal to a broad range of applications with large files requiring frequent alterations. W-O optical technology, on the other hand, has a loyal but smaller following of users needing data permanency more than flexibility.

Not only did many users have applications appropriate for rewritable optical technology, but also the W-O market initially was (it is no longer) a jumble of proprietary formats. Rather than contribute to that confusion, H-P chose to help push for standards for rewritable optical drives. Industry standard media allows for the transfer of data among different media and drive manufacturers. Also, media prices will eventually be lower if many manufacturers are making the same media. The rewritable optical standard is now well on its way with the Continuous Composite (CC) format in final approval by the International Organization for Standardization (ISO).

With rewritable optical standards in place, H-P has chosen to expand its optical technology to meet the needs of customers requiring the protection of W-O without sacrificing the advantages of widely accepted industry standards. In June 1990 a consortium of 14 companies, joining H-P, launched an effort to develop an optical technology that would allow drives to work with rewritable or W-O media. Rather than try to promote one of the many forms of write-once media already on the market, H-P took the existing widely accepted standard for magneto-optical (M-O) rewritable technology and applied it to W-O, so the two could coexist in a single drive.

A multifunction optical disk drive has a number of advantages. Over time, CC media costs will decline due to increased demand for standard media. Service and support and integration will be simpler and therefore less expensive. Also, software development time will be more rapid.

Multifunction optical products will serve the needs of users who already have applications for both W-O and rewritable, and those who anticipate beginning with one and growing into application areas that would require the other. Multifunction optical technology is also attractive to those whose files go through a lifecycle of change. For instance, a CAE drawing may need a series of alterations for which rewritable is the best solution, but the final design needs to be secured on W-O optical media.

H-P took extraordinary steps to meet the security needs required in W-O applications with a technology that also accommodates an alterable medium. The CC multifunction solution adapts existing rewritable media and drives for W-O applications, and incorporates multi-level safeguards in both the drive and media to protect the integrity of data. These protection measures are similar to protection measures used in other W-O optical technologies.

Write-once media protection measures include:
- factory codes
- disk initialization
- media certification

Write-once drive protection measures include:
- Data Management Pointers (DMP) inspection
- inspection of Error Correction Code (ECC) sample
- whole-block read with error correction

The next few sections of this chapter offer a detailed discussion of media and drive protection measures and the various ways they are implemented.

Media Protection Measures

Identifier codes and bytes help the multifunction optical disk drive distinguish between W-O and rewritable media and protect data integrity. Continuous Composite M-O media is manufactured with identifier codes molded into the disk's recording layer. These codes, known as the Phase Encoded Part (PEP) and the Standard Format Part (SFP), are reserved parts on the disk which contain data about the disk's geometry and permanently differentiate W-O media from rewritable media (see Figure 1). The multifunction drive checks the PEP and SFP codes to identify the media as either write-once or rewritable.

Disk Definition Structure (DDS) identifier bytes are written to the Continuous Composite W-O (CCW) media upon initialization. DDS bytes provide further information for media identification and prevention of overwrites.

Data recorded on CCW media is not likely to be lost because of defects in the media thanks to a certification process borrowed from rewritable CC media. Certification involves a rigorous check not only of data fields but also flag fields. During certification, the entire disk is screened for defects and all defective areas are permanently disabled to prevent future use. This certification provides a high level of media reliability and reduces the amount of defect management required during use.

Drive Protection Measures

In addition to media protection measures, this multifunction solution

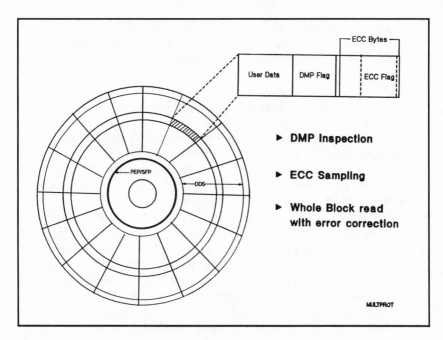

Figure 1. How it Works: Multilevel Protection Drive Protection Methods. Courtesy Hewlett-Packard Company.

implements a three-stage process to verify blank areas to which data may be written: data management pointer inspection, ECC checking, and whole-block read with error correction. This "blank checking" process is among the most thorough of any W-O drive, and because each check is invoked only if necessary, data integrity is not gained at the expense of performance.

When a data block is written, a 12-byte flag is set in the DMP bytes of the block. During blank checking, the presence of a flag signals that the data block has already received data; therefore the drive will not write in that block. The absence of a flag signals a blank block that is ready to accept data.

If the reading of the 12-byte DMP flag is marginal for any reason, the drive checks its next level of protection, a 12-byte sample protected by the ECC field. The ECC flag is also attached to every data block. Here again, the drive performs an inspection to verify whether it is looking at a written block or a blank block.

If the ECC flag inspection is marginal for any reason, the

drive performs its most detailed pass, a read with full error correction. In this final stage, the drive completes a full error correction pass on the data block and defines it clearly as either written or unwritten.

Putting Protective Measures in Place

How does all of this work in the process of reading and writing data? When optical media is loaded into a multifunction drive, the drive conducts spin-up and identifies the media. Once the multifunction optical disk drive recognizes the media, it enables the appropriate command set. If the PEP and SFP codes identify the media as W-O media, the drive invokes the W-O command set. If rewritable media is inserted, the drive invokes the rewritable command set. The W-O command set in this multifunction technology does not support destructive commands such as erase and reformat; thus once identified, W-O media cannot be altered as rewritable media. Similarly, when rewritable media is loaded and identified, the command set allows the drive to function in rewritable mode.

If CCW media is accidentally inserted in a CC rewritable drive, the non-multifunction drive will not recognize the media and therefore not access it; no reading or writing will occur.

The Drive for Industry Standards

H-P is taking a number of steps to bring about the second promise of this multifunction technology: industry standards. Already H-P has researched the appeal and technical feasibility of this approach among customers, industry experts, Original Equiptment Manufacturers (OEMs), media, system and drive manufacturers. The original fourteen companies and others have created a forum to discuss the technical specification drafted by H-P. Once finalized, the specification will be presented to the ANSI, ISO, and European Computer Manufacturers Association (ECMA) standards organizations as new project proposals. If accepted, the proposal will then begin the usual one-to-two year approval process.

Appendix 1. Proposed Draft Standard for Continuous Composite Write-once Media

Note: Developed in mid-1990 and sponsored by Hewlett-Packard Company, the following document is a proposed draft standard for "Continuous Composite Write-once Media" which is subject to change. This draft standard was presented at a Continuous Composite Write-once (CCW) public Optical Forum on September 14, 1990, at the Fairmont Hotel (San Jose, CA). Presenters included representatives from 3M, Sony Corporation, Freeman Associates, Inc., ENDL Associates, Maxoptix Corporation, and Hewlett-Packard Company.

Continuous Composite Write-once Media Specification

This document specifies the characteristics of 130mm Optical Disk Cartridges (ODC) of the type providing for information to be written once and read many times using magneto-optical (M-O) effects. It is based on the ISO DIS 10089A standard for rewritable optical disk cartridges using M-O effects. There are a few significant differences. All specifications and interchange requirements are exactly the same as DIS 10089A except those that are detailed in section II.

I. Principle

The following measures are implemented on M-O media to allow WRITE ONCE functionality:

1. The media type identifiers in the PEP and SFP control tracks are set to uniquely identify the disk as WRITE ONCE based on M-O effects.

2. The DDS identifiers in the Defect Management Area (DMA) are set to uniquely identify the disk as having been initialized for WRITE ONCE operations.

3. The 12 bytes in the data field designated as DMP bytes are not used in the rewritable disks but will be used as a flag to pre-

vent inadvertent write operations over previously written data.

Drives that use media conforming to this standard will be able to identify this media as WRITE ONCE based on M-O effects from the contents of PEP, SFP, and DDS. Other (existing rewritable) drives will be able to identify it as non-rewritable and reject it. The DDS identifiers will further indicate whether the disk has been initialized. The standard requires that the disk be initialized before user data is recorded on it.

The initialization can be with or without certification (as is ISO DIS 10089A). The option of write/read certification is unique to this WRITE ONCE implementation and offers added data integrity over other WORM type media. Further, the integrity of the 12 byte flag, reserved for written/blank status indication, is protected by ECC and may also be verified during certification.

At the end of the initialization process all sectors for data and spare areas are required to be pre-erased. So during normal write operations, an erase pass is not required. Sectors in the user area are either blank (erased) or written. If they are blank the 12 DMP bytes are unrecorded. If they are written, all of these bytes are set to (FF). The drive can use these bytes to disallow writing over previously written data.

Defect management is as in ISO DIS 10089A: Sector slipping during certification and linear replacement for grown defects. The SDL sectors are the only sectors on the disk that may be updated under internal drive control.

II.   Changes to ISO/IEC DIS 10089A

Text in bold print indicates a significant change from ISO/IEC DIS 100989A.

> *Sec 1 — line 1*

1.   Scope

This standard specifies the characteristics of 130mm optical disk cartridges (ODC) of the type providing for information to be **written once and read many times** using magneto-optical effects.

Sec 1 — line 9

(This standard specifies)

- The magneto-optical characteristics and recording character istics for recording the information once and for reading it many times, so as to provide physical interchangeablity between data processing systems.

- One format for the physical disposition of the tracks and sectors, the error corretion codes, the modulation methods used for the recording and the quality of signals.

Sec 7.2

(Definitions)

7.22 rewritable optical disk:

{Delete section. Instead add}

7.22 WRITE ONCE optical disk: An optical disk in which data in specified areas can be written only once and read many times.

Sec 10.12

(Write-inhibit holes—Second paragraph, First sentence)

When writing on Side A of the disk is not allowed, the write-inhibit hole shall be open all through the case.

(Write-inhibit holes—Fourth paragraph, First sentence)

When writing is allowed on Side A of the disk, the write-inhibit hole shall be closed on Side A of the case, at a depth of typically L(10), i.e. the wall thickness of the case.

Sec 16.4.3.1.1

Byte 7

The byte shall specify the media type

0001 0001 shall mean an optical disk according to this standard.

Sec 17.2.11.3

Sec 17.2.11.3—bytes for control information

This 12 byte (DMP) field is intended to prevent inadvertent write operations over previously written data. When the sector does not contain user data this field shall be unrecorded. When the sector does contain user data, the bytes of this field shall be set to (FF).

Sec 17.4.1.1

{Delete section. Instead add}

Sec 17.4.1.1—Media Initialization

The media shall be initialized only once. Once the DMAs are recorded, it indicates the disk is initialized and no further initialization of the disk is permitted. During media initialization, four DMAs are recorded. The user area is divided into groups, each containing data sectors and spare sectors. The spare sectors are used as replacements for defective data sectors. Media initialization can include a certification of the user area. **All data and spare sectors shall be in the erased (unrecorded) condition at the end of initialization.**

Sec 17.4.2

Write procedure

{Add}

User data shall always be recorded with DMP, CRC, and ECC as specified by this standard with a single pass write

operation (no erase pass). Erase conditions are not allowed in the user area after media initialization.

Sec 17.4.3.1—Table 5

Byte No	Description
0	**(05)** (DDS identifier MSB)
1	**(05)** (DDS identifier LSB)

Sec 18

Format B

{Delete}

Annex E

{Delete. Add instead}

Pointer Fields

The 12 bytes denoted by P(xy) in figure 10 & 11 shall be used to indicate whether or not a sector has been written. Each of these bytes shall be set to (FF) if the sector is written. If the sector is blank these bytes shall be unrecorded. These bytes follow the user data and are protected by ECC and CRC.

Annex H

Annex H (informative)

Sector retirement guidelines

{Add}

(e) The total number of bad bytes in the DMP fields exceeds 2.

III. Implications for drives using CONTINUOUS COMPOSITE WRITE ONCE media

1.   Read the PEP and/or SFP during spin-up to ascertain media type and enable/disable appropriate commands.

2.   Read DDS during spin-up to ascertain if the disc has been initialized. If it has, disallow re-initialization. If it has not been initialized, disallow access to the user area.

3.   Pre-erase the media before initialization is declared complete. The DDS sectors should be recorded only at the end of initialization to allow incomplete initialization to be detectable.

4.   Before writing to a sector, first ascertain whether the sector has already been written. This can be determined by inspecting the contents of the DMP bytes. If these are set to (FF), disallow writing the sector.

5.   Disallow commands that can directly or indirectly alter written data such as:

        1.   ERASE
        2.   REASSIGN BLOCKS
        3.   UPDATE BLOCK

6.   Prevent direct user access to the 12 DMP bytes. Disallow the WRITE LONG command. Always write user data with DMP, CRC and ECC as specified by the standard.

7.   The 12 DMP bytes provide the flag for blank checking. It is also possible to inspect the ECC fields to obtain an additional indication on whether or not a sector is blank. Further, a READ with ECC of the whole sector can be performed to determine whether the sector has been written. At Hewlett-Packard, we have found it advantageous to use all three methods in sequence as needed to optimize reliability and speed of this determination.

Optical Technology

The fourteen companies that originally joined H-P to announce the development of the CC multifunction optical disk drive standard are:

3M Company
Corporate Marketing Services
Building 225-35-05
3M Center
St. Paul, MN 55144-1000
612-733-7297
Fax: 612-736-3094

Asahi Chemical Industry Co. Ltd.
Information Processing Systems Division
Department of Optical Disks
The Imperial Tower
1-1, 1-Chome, Uchisaiwai-cho
Chiyoda-ku
Tokyo 100, Japan
81-3-507-2463
Fax: 81-3-508-1474

Daicel (USA), Inc.
23456 Hawthorne Bldg.
Bldg. #5, Suite #130
Torrance, CA 90505
213-791-2028
Fax: 213-791-2031

Fuji Photo Film Co. Ltd.
26-30 Nishiazabu 2-chome
Minato-ku, Tokyo, 106 Japan
81-3-486-6520
Fax: 81-3-406-2492

Kuraray Co., Ltd.
M-O Disk Promotion Department
Shin-Nihonbashi Building
3-8-2, Nihonbashi, Chuo-ku,
Tokyo 103 Japan

81-3-277-3363
Fax: 81-3-277-3320

Maxoptix Corporation
2520 Junction Ave.
San Jose, CA 95134
408-432-4482
Fax: 408-433-3321

Mitsui Petrochemical Industries, Ltd.
Memory Devices Department
Kasumigaseki Bldg.
P.O. Box 90
3-2-5 Kasumigaseki, Chiyoda-ku
Tokyo 100, Japan
81-3-580-1646
Fax: 81-3-593-0029

Nixdorf Computer AG
Product Division Open Systems
D-4790 Paderborn
West Germany
49-5251-10-3666
Fax: 49-5251-10-3350

Olympus Optical Company, Ltd.
Planning and Sales Section
Optical Memory Division
San-ei Building
22-2, Nishi-Shinjuku
1-chome, Shinjuku-ku
Tokyo, Japan
81-3-340-2270
Fax: 81-3-340-2201

Optical Storage Corporation
Akasaka Twin Tower (East) 16th Floor
2-17-22, Akasaka
Minatoku, Tokyo 107, Japan
81-3-583-3263
Fax: 81-3-583-3237

Philips and Du Pont Optical
1409 Foulk Road
Suite 200
Wilmington, DE 19803-0469
302-479-2507
Fax: 302-479-2512

Ricoh Corporation
Tenkoh 50 Bldg.
Mfg. Dept. #2
2-7-19 Shin-Yokohama, Kohoku-ku
Components Div.
Tokyo, 222 Japan
81-45-474-7375
Fax: 81-45-474-7377

Seiko Epson Corp.
OEM Project Suwaminami Branch
1010 Fijimi Fujimi-machi, Suwa-gun
Nagano-k`en, 399-02 Japan
81-266-62-6020
Fax: 81-266-62-5613

Sony Corporation
M-O Business Development Division
Storage Systems Group
Atsugi Technology Center #2
2255 Okata, Atsugi City
Kanagawa 243, Japan
81-462-27-2182
Fax: 81-462-27-2190

Chapter Three

Using Phase-Change Technology with Direct Overwrite in a Multifunction Optical Disk Drive

Anthony J. Jasionowski

At the June 1990 COMDEX Spring trade show, Panasonic (Matsushita Electric Industrial, Ltd. Co) introduced the world's first commercially available multifunction rewritable optical disk drive that uses a newly developed phase-change (P-C) technology with direct overwrite—the ability to rewrite data within a single pass of the optical head. Another multifunction optical disk drive, a dye polymer (D-P)/magneto-optic (M-O) technology which does have a direct overwrite feature, was also announced at COMDEX by Pioneer Communictions of America.

What Is a Multifunction Optical Disk Drive?

A single multifunction optical disk drive has the ability to use both rewritable and WORM media depending upon the application. Up to 1990, optical disk drives have been dedicated single-function devices—Read-Only Memory (ROM), Write-Once, Read-Many (WORM), or rewritable. The use of any of these three types of optical drives depends upon the application. CD-ROM is ideally suited for mass distribution of electronic data such as databases and reference materials as

26

well as software. WORM is best suited for archiving data while rewritable optical storage is being actively used as secondary, backup, and removable primary storage for PCs and workstations. The optical disk's characteristic of removability is superior to the common fixed magnetic hard disk drive in secure applications.

Some applications require the use of more than one type of drive, hence the need for a multifunction optical device. Today most computer users employ a combination of separate magnetic (fixed) rigid, (removable) flexible, and tape drives for obvious reasons. With the trend in downsizing (reflected by the explosive growth of the laptop, notebook, and desktop computer markets), the implementation and selection of mass storage devices is becoming increasingly critical to the success of future computer products and subsystems. For these reasons and others, small (5.25-inch footprint) optical disk drives will find their way into more and more PC and workstation applications.

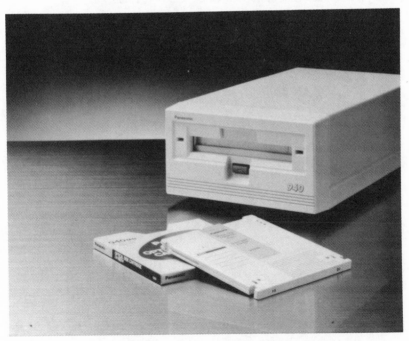

Figure 1. The LF-5010 WORM Optical Disk Drive. Courtesy Panasonic.

Figure 2. The LF-9000 Rewritable M-O Drive. Courtesy Panasonic.

Figure 3. The LF-7010 Multifunction Optical Disk Drive. Courtesy Panasonic.

Optical Disk Alternatives and Compatibility

CD-ROM is a reasonably well-standardized optical technology and is being used in a variety of operating environments including DEC, Sun, OS/2, Xenix, DOS, Macintosh, and Unix. *Most* CD-ROM discs produced today are readable on *most* CD-ROM drives produced by various manufacturers. CD-ROM drives are also the least expensive of the family of optical disk devices with prices ranging from $500 to $1,000.

WORM drives, on the other hand, are not as compatible since the technology, (e.g., recording mechanism [the method data is actually written onto the disk]) varies among drive manufacturers. For example, there exist several different recording mechanisms including ablative and non-ablative WORM media. WORM drives could be made compatible at the unrecorded level; however, the written data or logical format could vary depending on the drive's software which could mean incompatibility of the recorded (written) disks.

There is a proposed standard for rewritable optical to which several companies including Panasonic adhere. The International Organization for Standardization (ISO) and the American National Standards Institute (ANSI) have been diligent in their efforts to develop several proposed WORM and rewritable optical media standards. Panasonic and its parent company, Matsushita Electric Industrial, have been active participants in both ANSI and ISO. Recently, there has been discussion and consideration of multifunctionality as it relates to both full and partial ROM as well as WORM (in other words, a rewritable disk with a predefined area for ROM and/or WORM); however, it is too early to predict the outcome of these discussions.

Multifunction Optical Disk Drives: Choices

As previously mentioned, due to the distinct and dissimilar technologies used by various optical drive manufacturers, and in order to have ensured backward compatibility with current WORM drive product lines, three different approaches to multifunction optical storage have emerged in first-generation drives; dye-polymer/M-O utilized by Pioneer, Continuous Composite Write-Once (CCW) implemented by H-P, Sony, and a consortium of over a dozen other companies, and phase-change with direct overwrite developed by Panasonic, LMSI, and Optimem.

Approach 1. Dye-Polymer/M-O Multifunction Optical Storage

D-P technology has been used for the past several years by several WORM drive manufacturers. However, due to difficulty in developing a rewritable D-P system, a different approach has been developed combining D-P (for WORM) with M-O technology and media (for rewritability) in a multifunction optical disk drive. Since early proponents of dye-polymer favored the Sampled Servo (SS) format rather than the optical industry's more common and popular Continuous Composite (CC) format, the D-P multifunction approach uses a SS format. This, in turn, makes this particular rewritable M-O media incompatible with proposed ANSI standards for rewritable optical media. The current nature of rewritable M-O does not allow direct overwrite and this type of system also has a limited storage capacity per disk side.

Approach 2. Continuous Composite (CCW)/M-O Multifunction Optical Storage

For the most part, the proponents (a consortium of fourteen companies) of CCW are manufacturers of optical disk drives and media, some of which do not currently offer 5.25-inch WORM drives or media. Since there is an existing market for WORM and, more important, a developing market for multifunction optical disk drives, this group has concluded that it is wise to use the same rewritable M-O media but only in a "WORM-only" mode. This is accomplished by writing a special signal onto the control tracks of the M-O media at the time of media manufacture. This signal would be detected by the multifunction drive identifying it as a WORM disk rather than rewritable disk despite the fact that it is actually M-O rewritable media. Simply stated, CCW is rewritable media disguised as WORM.

Approach 3. Phase-Change Multifunction Optical Storage

From the outset, Panasonic has pursued a totally different route from that of the above approaches. In 1963 Panasonic began development of optical recording materials and since the late 1960s has been the forerunner in the development of P-C optical storage technology. In 1980 Panasonic introduced a WORM videodisc and in 1985 and 1987 introduced, respectively, 8- and 5.25-inch phase-change WORM media and drives.

In 1983 Panasonic demonstrated the first rewritable P-C videodisc using a two-beam system (separate erase and write passes). Introduced in 1989, Panasonic's current WORM P-C drive is ranked second in the 5.25-inch WORM market with a thirty three percent market share according to Dataquest.

P-C is a non-ablative (no physical change) recording system based on the amorphous/crystalline transition of tellurium-based thin films. It was first used by Panasonic in both analog (video) and data storage WORM drives since the cyclability of the early materials was limited. Cyclability is the number of times that the media can be repeatedly erased and rewritten. Since the initially developed rewritable optical materials were limited to less than 100,000 cycles, a very vigorous phase-change media was first developed by Panasonic exclusively for WORM applications. This WORM phase-change media has been in actual use for the past ten years.

Phase-Change Rewritable Optical Technology

With the success of WORM P-C, Panasonic endeavored to improve the cyclability of rewritable phase-change optical media. Figure 4 demonstrates that there is no appreciable increase in errors up to 300,000 overwrite cycles. Also, the crystallization speed of earlier rewritable phase-change materials was too slow and consequently required a dual-beam system (one for erasing and the other for writing).

Today, Panasonic has achieved a single-beam rewritable P-C system with direct overwrite. This was achieved by the development of improved P-C media featuring a shorter crystallization time of less than 50ms compared to 200ms in the past. To write, erase, and read data on rewritable P-C optical media, a focussed laser beam is irradiated onto the active (recording) layer of the disk. As shown in Figure 5, by modulating the power of a single semiconductor, laser-writing, erasing, or reading can be easily controlled depending upon the laser power level.

A higher power level of about 20mW, which exceeds the melting temperature of the active layer, is used for writing the (less reflective) amorphous marks representing the written data which, in turn, is read using the same laser but at a much lower power of about 1-2mW. The read-out signal is obtained from the difference of the reflectivities of the written (less reflective amorphous) and unwritten or erased (more reflective crystallized) areas of the track. An intermediate pow-

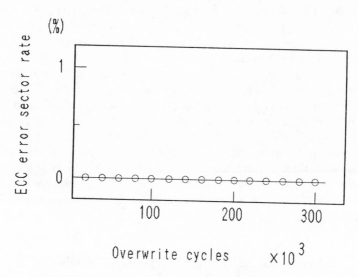

Figure 4. Cyclability of Phase-Change Media. Courtesy Panasonic.

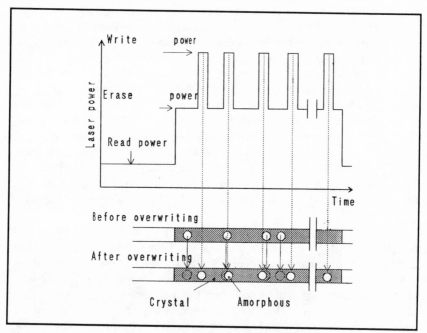

Figure 5. Single-Beam Overwrite. Courtesy Panasonic.

er level of about 9-10mW is used to erase (crystallize) the previously written (amorphous) marks.

Rewritable P-C drives use a single laser to erase and write data at the same time within a single pass of the optical head which provides faster overall system performance. The use of a magnetic field and subsequent separate pass for erasing is not required as it is with current rewritable M-O drives. Since the same erasing and writing mechanism is used in P-C, it is relatively easy to define a multifunction optical phase-change drive with direct overwrite and backward compatibility with Panasonic's current 940MB WORM media. In fact, Panasonic's new multifunction optical disk drive (Model LF-7010) uses the same basic optical head as the LF-5010 WORM drive except that the semiconductor laser is of a higher output power (namely, 40mW versus 30mW, maximum rated output power). A block diagram of Panasonic's multifunction optical disk drive is shown in Figure 6 .

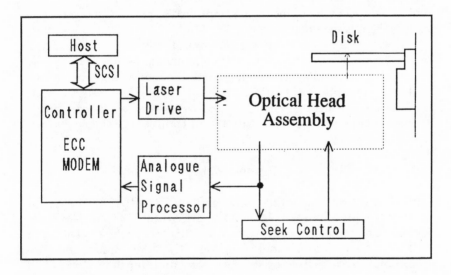

Figure 6. Block Diagram of LF-7010, Panasonic's Multifunction Optical Disk Drive. Courtesy Panasonic.

To date, the basic criticism of rewritable P-C technology concerns media cyclability as compared to M-O. Typically, today's rewritable M-O provides one million write/erase/rewrite cycles. Panasonic has developed rewritable P-C media which will also provide one million cycles when installed in its multifunction optical disk drive through the use of a defect management scheme that automatically monitors the media for defects and ensures complete data integrity for the user.

All optical disks including ROM, WORM, and rewritable have errors that are inherent in the design and manufacture of the media. Therefore, it is necessary to incorporate an error detection and correction (EDC) circuit in all optical disk drives used for data storage. In the case of WORM and rewritable optical disks, a defect management scheme is also used to compensate for defective sectors (a finite area usually 256, 512, 1K, or 2K bytes of data) on the disk. If a sector is found to be defective before or after the data is written, the defective sector is flagged as defective and it is replaced by a good spare sector elsewhere on the disk. In the case of rewritable P-C media, defective sectors occur due to the usual media defects as well as media degradation caused by excessive overwrite cycles (more 100,000 cycles). Panasonic's defect management scheme used in the LF-7010 ensures that the logical cyclability of the data is improved to more than one million cycles which is the same for rewritable M-O.

The Panasonic multifunction optical disk drive can read and write Panasonic's current 940MB WORM media as well as the new 1GB rewritable media. For even greater storage capacity, up to two multifunction optical disk drives can be installed into Panasonic's current automatic cartridge changer (jukebox) which can be configured with any combination of up to fifty WORM and/or rewritable disks.

Conclusion

Panasonic expects to continue offering the LF-5010 WORM drive for archiving applications which ranges in price from $3,000 to $4,500; rewritable drives start at $4,500 while multifunction drives start at about $5,000. In the near term, single-function WORM, rewritable, and multifunction drives will co-exist; however, multifunction drives will eventually have an impact on single-function drives as manufacturing cost differences are reduced with volume production over the next few years.

The advantages of Panasonic's P-C multifunction drive are apparent in terms of cost/performance. Panasonic offers the highest capacity (940MB to 1GB) of any multifunction optical disk drive. Panasonic is committed to offering a full line of optical disk drives and for this reason it has also introduced an ANSI/ISO proposed-standard rewritable M-O disk drive (LF-9000) for applications that require only rewritability and compatibility with the proposed standard.

As a result of this product announcement, Panasonic expects renewed industry interest in the further research and development of P-C technology permitting even greater capacities and performance as well as the potential for compatibility with full and partial ROM, providing the ultimate in multifunction optical disk drives. In addition to data storage applications, P-C optical technology is also applicable to both analog audio and video storage as evidenced by Panasonic's twelve-inch WORM drive capable of storing 600 High-Definition TV (HDTV) images.

Chapter Four

Answering the Need for WORM and Rewritable Optical Storage: The Multifunction Optical Disk Drive

Kent F. Ekberg, Richard Miller, and Cris Simpson

Pioneer Communications of America became the first company to ship a mass-produced multifunction (rewritable/WORM [write-once, read-many]) optical disk drive in 1990. Pioneer has been selling 130mm (5.25-inch) WORM drives for over two years. Until 1990 optical technology users were forced to use separate WORM drives for storing information on a more permanent, long-term basis, or rewritable magneto-optical (M-O) for storing large amounts of information that will change. Introduced at the Spring 1990 COMDEX, Pioneer's multifunction drive answers the need for both WORM and M-O rewritable optical data storage because it can host both types of media. Its multifunctionality is based on the use of the Sampled Servo (SS) format for both types of optical storage media.

Justification for Multifunction Optical Storage

Multifunction optical disk drives can archive files on WORM disks,

Figure 1. Rewritable/WORM Multifunction Optical Disk Drive (DE-U2001 and 5.25-inch Rewritable Optical Disk. Courtesy Pioneer Communications of America, Inc.

providing long life, permanence, and comparatively inexpensive cost. At the same time, multifunction optical disk drives offer the use of M-O disks which are easily integrated into a system and are erasable, rewritable, and can readily handle dynamic files. Once files with dynamic information need to be stored permanently, they can be copied onto a WORM disk. For example, in CAD/CAM applications working drawings might be stored on M-O while they are in the development stages; when they are completed, they can be copied onto WORM.

The same process could be employed for electronic publishing files: M-O can be used for working documents and WORM for archiving the finished documents. In fact, the multifunction drive could be used in a similar way for transaction processing in financial applications, image storage and retrieval, medical imaging, government archiving, and other data-intensive applications.

Obviously, not all records need the long-term archiveability of WORM. In these applications, the ability to reuse the cartridges provides substantial cost savings. Those records that need to be kept or protected can then be copied to WORM media. The multifunction drive allows the user to perform these tasks without purchasing two different optical disk drives.

Pioneer's systems conform to the SS format allowing the company's multifunction drive (DE-7001) to maintain downward compatibility with Pioneer's DD-5001 series of WORM optical disk drives. The DE-7001 drives can read and write any media used in the DD-5001 drives, and the media can be used in DD-5001 drives too. This preserves the investment that users have made in Pioneer's WORM products, including hardware, software, media, data files, and user training. The multifunction drive is a good choice for companies now getting involved with optical storage since it allows them to put off the WORM/rewritable decision indefinitely.

Pioneer's Multifunction Optical Storage Technology

Pioneer's WORM media is based on an organic dye. For data writes, a semiconductor laser at a power level of 10 to 13mW is used to "ablate" or burn pits into the organic dye. Later, the laser is also used to read the disk since the pits have a lower reflectivity than the non-ablative areas. WORM media conforms to the International Organization for Standardization (ISO)/IS 9171 (Format B) standard.

M-O media and data read/write methods are considerably more complex. M-O disks are made from a magnetic thin film of a rare earth-transition metal alloy. To write, the laser is used not to ablate the material, but to heat it to its Curie point, the temperature at which it loses its coercive magnetic field. As the laser is turned off, the material cools and takes the magnetic orientation of the ambient magnetic field generated by a coil just above the media. Writing is a two-pass process, requiring a pass for North and one for South orientation. To read the data, the laser is used at a much lower power level. The laser is reflected off of the media to a polarizing beam splitter. Due to the Kerr effect, the plane of polarization of the reflected light is rotated one way or the other, depending on the magnetic orientation. Although this rotation is minute (0.01 radians either way), it forms the basis for M-O storage. Pioneer's rewritable M-O media conforms to ISO/DIS 10089 (Format B).

Sampled Servo Format

Pioneer has opted to design multifunction optical disk drives that conform to the SS format because it has several advantages over the Continuous Composite Servo System (CCS):

- The data and servo areas are separate assuring a higher Signal-to Noise Ratio (SNR) because there is no crosstalk between the data and servo areas. The controller circuitry required of SS only is simpler because the controller has to do one thing at a time—tracking, focus, or data.

- SS media is grooveless, making it easier to manufacture. The lack of groove/data pit crosstalk improves both the data SNR and the tracking accuracy.

- The higher SNR allows the drive to handle a wider variety of media types, as well as making it less sensitive to manufacturing variations in the media.

- SS will make higher-density formats possible while retaining compatibility concomitant with Pioneer's commitment to a migration path and long-term support.

Sampled Servo Compared with Continuous Composite

The main difference between SS and the CCS format is how the tracking information is placed on the optical media. CCS uses grooves, much like a phonograph record, with the data written on the higher "land" between the "valleys." A three-beam optical system is required, with one beam for the data, and two for tracking the grooves. The optical system is continuously handling focus, tracking, and data. One problem with CCS is that the tracking system can mistake data pits as grooves. Mistracking causes crosstalk between data pits and grooves. Focusing is also more difficult due to the changing diffraction patterns caused by the pits and grooves.

SS solves these problems by separating the tracking, focus, and data operations in time and space. SS media has no grooves, but when it is created, it is pre-formatted with a set of wobble pits that are used for the tracking servo. The wobble pits are offset from the (imaginary) centerline by approximately one-quarter track pitch. Each track is broken into 32 sectors, and each sector is broken into 43 data areas comprised of a two-byte servo area and 16 bytes of data.

The media's rotation brings the servo area under the laser

first. As the beam moves between the wobble pits, the servo system compares the relative amplitudes of the (lack of) reflection from each pit. When the tracking is correct, the amplitudes will be equal. Next, the beam moves through a mirror area used for focusing. This area is free of pits to allow for the most accurate focusing. After the focus area is a single clock pit, which is used to measure rotation speed and to mark the beginning of the data pits. The data area is 16 bytes long. After the data pits come the servo bytes for the next data area. This cycle of tracking adjustment, focus, and data operations occurs approximately 1,400 times per media revolution.

In 1990 five other companies announced their support for the ISO (Format B) SS drives manufactured by Pioneer. Laser Magnetic Storage International (LMSI) and Optimem, two leading optical disk drive manufacturers, announced their intention to begin sales of compatible drives. Optical Storage Corporation, Pioneer, Philips & Du Pont Optical (PDO), as well as TDK have announced their plans to produce compatible media for Pioneer's optical disk drives. These companies will continue to work together to ensure that compatibility is achieved among their products whenever possible, to help bring to market in the future new products with greater speeds and capacities.

Everything is the same except the servo differences. The SS format makes the development of a highly reliable separated optical system possible. As seen in Figure 3, only the objective lens, mirror, and focussing actuator move from track to track. The 825nm laser diode, photodetectors, and other lenses are fixed.

Inner Workings of the Multifunction Optical Disk Drive

Optical drives typically have slower access times than magnetic drives due to the weight of the moving element. In the past, M-O drives have had particularly slow access times due to the complexity of the optical head. The separated optical system of Pioneer's multifunction optical disk drive, the DE-7001, allows average seek times (1/3 stroke) of 53mS. The objective lens assembly is moved by a linear motor for gross tracking, while fine tracking adjustment is achieved with a 2-D voice coil. The voice coil can move the objective lens up and down for focusing, and side-to-side (perpendicular to the track) for fine tracking. SS allows the use of a single beam pickup because there are no grooves to follow as there are in CCS systems.

Focus error is detected using an astigmatism method. One of

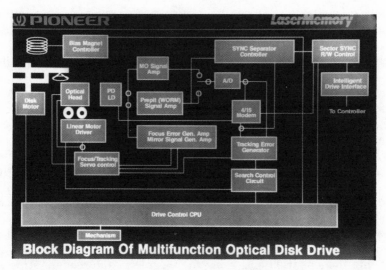

Figure 2. Block Diagram of Multifunction Optical Disk Drive. Courtesy Pioneer
Communications of America.

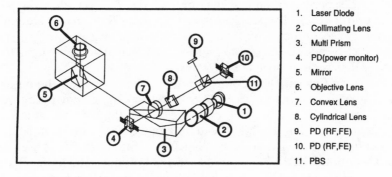

Figure 3. Configuration of the Optical Head. Courtesy Pioneer Communications of
America.

the advantages of the SS format is that focusing is performed only in
the mirror region of the servo area. Because of this, there are none of
the changes in diffraction patterns seen with CCS. Astigmatism is generated by a cylindrical lens in the return light path before the polariz-

ing beam splitter. The focus error signal is generated by a quadrature photodetector.

The controller circuitry for the multifunction optical disk drive is divided between two boards. The Mechanical Unit Controller Board (MUCB) handles all of the analog control and data functions, while the optical disk controller handles the digital functions such as error correction and Small Computer System Interface (SCSI) protocol.

The main task of the MUCB is to convert the RF signal from the photodetectors to a digital data stream for the optical disk controller. The MUCB also handles all of the analog feedback from the laser head and disk motor. The optical head is adjusted for tracking and focus by the MUCB at every data area. This is accomplished by feeding the error signal returned from the quadrant detector through the focus servo control to maintain both focus and tracking. Since the optical head has a peak dynamic range of about 25 tracks, it does not need to be moved for a short seek. The short seek can be accomplished by just moving the lens itself and using the wobble pits to realign. This allows a track-to-track seek time of less than 2ms.

The MUCB is also responsible for amplifying the difference between signals from the photodetectors when in M-O mode or the amplitude signal when in WORM mode. This signal is sent to both the sync separator/timing generator and the A/D (analog/digital) Convertor (ADC). The ADC which converts the RF signal to a digital stream is synchronized by the sync separator/timing generator. The MUCB also codes the signal to an RLL 4/15 format and maintains the proper disk rotation speed of 1800 rpm.

The Optical Disk Controller (ODC) handles all of the digital functions for the drive such as SCSI handshaking, command decoding, command execution, and returning data to the host machine. The ODC is based on the NEC V40 microprocessor, an Intel 80286-compatible. The ODC contains 256KB of working RAM, as well as 256KB of buffer RAM per attached mechanical unit. The buffer RAM is divided into two 128KB parallel buffers. Information is passed between the MUCB and the ODC through an Intelligent Drive Interface (IDI) bus.

This Pioneer proprietary interface was developed for internal use within optical drives and is also used in the company's series of WORM drives. The bus allows four mechanical units to be connected to one ODC board if additional controller RAM is installed. The MUCB is given a unique identification number through dip switches on the mechanical unit's controller board. These IDI identification numbers correspond to the MUCB's SCSI Logical Unit Number

(LUN). The Pioneer multifunction optical disk drive uses the industry standard SCSI interface. The full-height internal drive has an embedded SCSI controller and a single internal SCSI connector. The external drive subsystem has two SCSI connectors for daisy chain operation.

The multifunction optical disk drive has two different modes of operation: rewritable and WORM. The default mode is set at start-up by a dip switch, but the mode may be changed at any time under software control. In WORM mode, the drive emulates a Pioneer DD-5001 series drive down to the SCSI INQUIRY data. This allows current WORM device drivers to operate without modification. In WORM mode, the ERASE and FORMAT commands will cause an INVALID COMMAND error. To handle the various modes, Pioneer introduced the vendor-unique SCSI commands READ MODE and CHANGE MODE.

The SCSI extended error codes do not provide a way to handle media/mode mismatches, such as WORM media being inserted while the drive is in rewritable mode. To address this, Pioneer introduced a vendor-unique extended sense code (83h) which is generated at the first SCSI command after the incorrect media is inserted. Pioneer made the decision to require the host to issue the CHANGE MODE command so that the device drivers will always know the current mode of the drive. This is critical to assure that the data integrity of the cartridge is maintained.

As noted earlier, the Pioneer multifunction optical disk drive conforms to the ISO/IS 9171 (Format B) for WORM disks and ISO/DIS 10089 (Format B) for M-O disks. Disk storage capacity is 327MB per disk side for a total of 654MB per cartridge. The average seek time is 53ms with an average latency of 16.7ms. Thus, the average access time is 69.7ms. Start-up time from disk insertion is 3.9 seconds, and stop time is 2.5 seconds. The drive's maximum burst data transfer rate is 1.5MBs; the maximum sustained data transfer rate is 491KBs. The drive's corrected bit error rate is 10^{-12} or less.

Interface kits for the IBM-PC/AT/XT, PS/2, Macintosh, and other popular platforms are becoming available from Pioneer and other third-party vendors including Computer Upgrade Corporation, a distributor of the multifunction optical disk drive.

The Future of Multifunction Optical Disk Drive

Pioneer expects the multifunction optical disk drive to be well received in the optical jukebox market where it can replace a WORM drive and a rewritable drive at the cost of the rewritable drive alone. Wherever a WORM drive is being used, a multifunction drive can be used. Wherever an M-O drive is being used, a multifunction optical disk drive can be used. There is also an interesting subset of applications yet to be discovered where only a multifunction drive will suffice. These are applications that system integrators and current optical storage and prospective end-users will begin to develop with the new device.

Currently, Pioneer is developing multifunction optical disk drives with higher capacities, faster access times, greater transfer rates, and the ability to use different media types. The SS format will allow these functions to be implemented without sacrificing downward compatibility with current products. Pioneer intends to continue to develop and support the SS format and to use it to develop new and innovative optical products.

Chapter Five

Rewritable Media Manufacturing for Multifunctional Optical Disk Drives

John J. Stevens

Optical technology is having a significant impact on data storage for libraries, government, industry, and business organizations throughout the world. In recordable media, the first answer for long-term data storage came in the form of write-once, read-many (WORM) drives and media which stored data safely and permanently. In 1990 rewritable optical media offered prospective end-users and system integrators flexible data and image updating and information replacement.

As much as both WORM and rewritable optical disk drives and media have begun to significantly change information storage today, the future may very well lie with multifunctionality. *Optical Memory News* published by Rothchild Consultants dubbed 1990 as "the year of the Rewritable drive." Perhaps 1991 will be proclaimed the "year of the Multifunction drive."

With this type of focus on multifunctionality by drive and media manufacturers, significant changes and progress are being made daily in this area. For instance, Philips and Du Pont Optical (PDO) is working with several drive companies (Laser Magnetic Storage International [LMSI], Optimem, and Pioneer) developing media for multifunction optical disk drives. While readers are probably familiar with multifunctionality from the drive perspective, there are some interesting details to consider from the media manufacturer's perspective. New products are developed and media manufacturers like PDO must be innovative and must lead in the perfection of the manufacturing process in order to form successful partnerships.

Formed in 1986, PDO is a joint venture between N.V. Philips, an inventor of optical storage technology, and Du Pont, a major materials manufacturer that serves many industries including the electronics industry. In the optical media, two years is the equivalent of two hundred years because technology, applications, uses, and businesses change so quickly. PDO manufactures five basic optical products: CD-audio, CD-ROM, videodisc, write-once (W-O), and rewritable optical media.

To understand multifunctionality and the role media plays, it is important to understand first the manufacturing process of rewritable optical media. A number of intricate steps are involved in the manufacturing of magneto-optic (M-O) rewritable media to ensure high-quality disks. This chapter is a "walk-through" of this process.

Figure 1. 5.25-inch Rewritable M-O Optical Disk and Cartridge. Courtesy Philips and Du Pont Optical Company.

Manufacturing M-O Disks

Ninety-nine percent of the manufacturing procedure takes place in a clean room environment; the robotics are fascinating. Staff must be very dedicated and technically skilled in order to perfect the process. One can conceptualize rewritable optical disks as floppy disks with extremely high data storage capacity. There are very demanding standards placed on rewritable optical media manufacturers. Obviously, only those with sufficient experience, resources and dedication are likely to succeed in becoming major media manufacturers.

In the rewritable optical disk manufacturing process, PDO uses M-O technology, which is the most common rewritable technology currently available. PDO believes it will remain the dominant rewritable optical technology for some time.

M-O has emerged as the leading rewritable optical technology for several reasons. It combines the best of both worlds by allowing focused laser energy for high-density recording and magnetic technology to change the polarity of a disk during writing and erasing cycles. This allows the life-cycle of the disk to reach 10 to the 8th power, far greater than the typical erase cycles of phase-change (P-C) or dye polymer (D-P) optical technologies. The second reason M-O is preferred is because the technology has matured faster than either D-P or P-C. Finally, this method is easily accepted because of the similarities with regular magnetic disks.

One essential step in the manufacture of any rewritable optical disk is to select the format to be used. There are several types of formatting but the two most common are Continuous Composite Servo (CCS) and Sampled Servo (SS); these two differ primarily in the way the drive looks for data stored on an M-O disk.

The next step in making a disk is to replicate the format information onto the substrate. The substrate can be glass or plastic. If a glass substrate is used, a photopolymer or 2P layer is spun onto a cleaned glass disk. Then a stamper embosses the information into the 2P layer. The disk is exposed to ultraviolet light which polymerizes the 2P making the embossed data permanent. If a plastic substrate is desired, the stamper is placed in an injection molding machine. The molten plastic conforms to the image of the stamper. The substrate is now ready for the next step.

The substrates enter a vacuum chamber to have several layers of thin films, called the stack, sputter-deposited onto them. It is here that the disk receives its M-O layers that will allow high-reliability read, write, and erase capabilities. Minute contaminants can completely ruin the disk at this stage. The first layer is a dielectric layer used to insulate the disk, protect it, and provide for optical enhancement.

Next, the M-O recording layer is added. This layer is the key to the disk's quality and reliability. An aluminum reflective layer is added as the third step in the sputtering process. Later, the reflectivity of the disk will be tested to be sure it meets the reflection levels necessary for laser drives.

The fourth step in the sputtering process is the addition of another dielectric layer to protect against oxidation. After another inspection to ensure adherence between the layers, the final lacquer layer is added for protection.

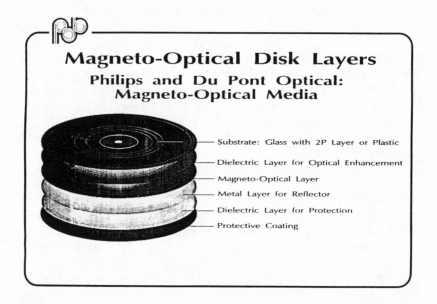

Figure 2. Layers of Magneto-Optical Media. Courtesy Philips and Du Pont Optical.

If this single-sided disk passes the reflectivity test, as well as basic M-O tests, it will be bonded to another half-disk and a hub will be installed.

Over twenty inspections and tests are performed before the disk is labelled. These occur at substrate development, washing, priming, replication, sputtering, hub installation, bonding of the disk, testing, and packaging and labelling. All of these are part of the quality assurance process. Testing throughout the manufacturing process allows corrections to be made to "get the disk back on track" if possible and ensure disk quality. Specially designed equipment checks every vital characteristic of the disk including imbalance, axial deviation, thickness, tilt, radial acceleration, and track eccentricity.

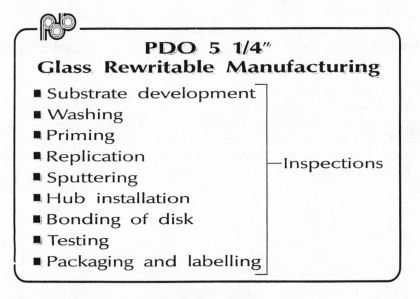

Figure 3. 5.25-inch Glass Rewritable Manufacturing. Courtesy Philips and Du Pont Optical Company.

For final testing, a machine specially designed and used by PDO runs the disk through eight key tests including sensitivity, write, erase, read, focus, and polarization. If the disk falls within certain strict parameters, it goes on to be packaged and labelled.

Functional performance in a drive is best accomplished in customer drives. PDO's glass rewritable disks have been qualified by the three leading manufacturers of rewritable drives, all of which conform to International Organization for Standardization (ISO) standards: Maxoptix (May 1988), Ricoh (June 1989), and Sony (November 1989). Industry standards are extremely important and PDO actively participates in this development. Often, PDO uses customer drives as a final functional test. Many customers prefer to have media supplied to them already formatted to ISO standards.

From Rewritable to Multifunctionality

Having a perspective on rewritable media manufacturing is only part of the journey in understanding the drive-media relationship in multi-functionality. There are many additional considerations. PDO has announced media support for multifunction drives from Hewlett-Packard Company (H-P), LMSI, Optimem, and Pioneer. The basic M-O coating, disk structure, and packaging are similar for all three but these drives (SS and CC) require optical media that is different in two important ways. The pre-formatted information is different and each requires its own drive for testing. LMSI, Optimem, and Pioneer are advocates of the SS format; H-P and Sony Corporation use the CC format.

Currently, PDO manufactures both formats: the ISO standard SS W-O media that plays in the LMSI, Optimem, and Pioneer drives, and the ISO standard CC M-O media for the H-P and Sony drives. To complete this family, PDO will add SS M-O for LMSI and Pioneer, and CC M-O media specially designed to work only in a W-O mode for H-P. Although this is not in the ISO standards yet, H-P and others are

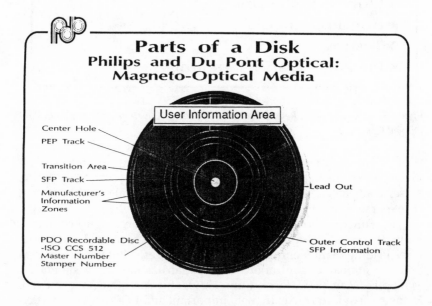

Figure 4. Parts of an M-O Disk. Courtesy Philips and Du Pont Optical Company.

dedicated to that end (see Chapters 1 and 2); PDO is supporting their efforts.

Because of PDO's prior experiences, the firm is familiar and experienced with SS and CC formats. Nevertheless, each new master type has its own learning curve. It is important to be very focused to create an electrical signal that will tune a laser recorder in such a way to create a physical replica on a disk of the format pattern. The header information in a few tracks of a CCS formatted disk is about two thousandths of an inch wide. It is important that this information be replicated in each disk in the same identical manner. SS media has a different format type but its pre-formatted information must also be precisely placed within tight tolerances.

Media for multifunction optical disk drives require modified masters in some cases. This adds to a media manufacturer's stamper requirements. Also, since PDO believes that functional testing on customer drives is important, it is adding to its drive-testing capability where required.

Conclusion

The multifunction optical disk drive adds a new dimension to the optical industry's offering and will help it move down the cost performance curve to provide an even better value to its customers. As media manufacturers' total sales volume increases, reductions in cost should allow PDO and other media firms to pass along economies-of-scale savings in multifunctionality.

Chapter Six

Software Considerations for Rewritable and Multifunction Optical Drives*

Brian A. Berg

A lthough the software development effort required for rewritable optical disk drives is less complex than that of write-once, read-many (WORM) drives, the characteristics of currently available rewritable optical disk technology invoke special concerns for integrators. Optical storage standards, magneto-optical (M-O) media, and the recent availability of phase-change (P-C) media and multifunction optical disk drives also present software integration and performance issues that must be understood in order to create an efficient and adaptable product.

Software for WORM versus Rewritable Media

To appreciate the software integration complexities of WORM optical devices, it is best to compare these drives with their rewritable optical counterparts. The best way to make this comparison is to look at the

---

*This chapter was originally published in the November/December 1990 issue of *Optical Information Systems*. It is reprinted with revisions.

rate at which these two optical disk drive types have penetrated the market.

Although WORM drives became available in 1984 and 1985, sales of this high-capacity random access device have always lagged projections. Even though WORM's non-volatility had a definite appeal to some market segments, support software was slow to emerge. Rewritable optical disk drives finally became available in mid-1988 following years of expectation and vaporware. Unlike WORM, rewritable drive integrators have been quick to release software packages for the major computer platforms.

The primary reason for the faster acceptance of rewritable drives as compared with write-once (W-O) is clear: *The W-O nature of WORM media creates a difficult software integration task in a world where most popular operating systems assume the use of a directly rewritable media for the storage of data files.*

While WORM technology has satisfied the needs of many users who required a high-capacity and removable random access media, its W-O characteristic has been a burden to some users. Although many predict its demise, WORM technology has found a market niche with users who require data security. Many users who are not concerned about non-volatility, but still require a high-capacity, removable media are now using rewritable devices.

Comparing Rewritable Optical Storage Technologies

Since rewritable optical media is indeed just that—rewritable—its integration is a far simpler chore since it can generally be used just like the well entrenched magnetic drives. All rewritable drives on the market used M-O technology until Panasonic announced its P-C multifunction optical disk drive in mid-1990. Another technique using organic dye-polymer (D-P) media was originally thought to have promise for rewritable devices, but it now appears destined only for write-once usage (WORM drives from Pioneer and Ricoh use D-P media). While the Canon M-O, Panasonic P-C, and Ricoh D-P drives do not use American National Standards Institute (ANSI)/International Organization for Standardization (ISO) standard media, virtually all other rewritable drives do.

M-O has the unique but unfortunate requirement that sectors must be erased before they are written, and currently all drives perform this erasure on a separate pass over the media. However, since P-C devices are directly rewritable (they permit new data to be written over old data in a single pass), they would appear to have a performance advantage.

Unlike M-O, P-C media is written by changing the morphological structure of the optical disk. This fact limits the number of rewrite cycles that the media can endure. Thus, prudence dictates that data be verified after it is written. Because verification involves a separate pass over the media, P-C and M-O both require two media passes for data to be written in an assured manner.

Although P-C's requirement for a verify pass over the media may be questioned by some, WORM drives have typically performed this verify function by default. Typically, M-O optical disk drives do not perform a verify pass since media is verified at format time and writing does not involve a structural change of the disk material.

In anticipation of P-C media sectors failing, the Panasonic multifunction optical disk drive allows the user to declare an area of the disk to be monitored for the number of times its sectors are written. Any such sector that is written $300,000^2$ times (this number is subject to change) is automatically remapped to a "spare" area. If it is written another 300,000 times, it is remapped again. However, if this happens again (after a total of 900,000 writes to the logical sector), an error will result. As most file systems require a disk's lowest numbered sectors to be rewritten the most often, this area is typically the one that would need to be monitored by the drive's firmware.

Mitigating Poor Performance

Since a two-pass write operation is a fact of life for current rewritable optical disk technology, the software integrator should attempt to minimize its impact. As the P-C verify pass must be performed before the write operation can be considered complete, there appears to be no way to improve P-C write performance. An M-O write operation, however, would require only one pass when a sector is requested to be written. This will be true if the following assumptions are made:

1. A newly formatted disk is always totally erased.

2. The drive's firmware has an ERASE command and its WRITE command has an Erase By-Pass (EBP) option.

3. Disk sectors are erased during the time between when they are de-allocated from one file and re-allocated to another file. If the first assumption is not already addressed by the drive's

internal format command, a utility could be easily written to erase disks before they are considered available for use.

The second assumption is addressed by the new Small Computer System Interface (SCSI)-2 standard, and virtually all rewritable optical drives are available with an SCSI interface.

The third assumption requires that a list of sectors be erased and a list of sectors already erased be maintained by the operating system or a system utility, and that these lists are written to a special area on each disk. When sectors are erased, sector numbers are moved from the to-be-erased list to the already-erased list. Under multitasking operating systems such as UNIX, OS/2, and DEC-VMS, sector erasure could be performed periodically by a "background" utility as well as when a disk is dismounted. A TSR (Terminate and Stay Resident) program can perform this chore under MS-DOS, although a special utility to mount and dismount media would also be needed to ensure the two lists are flushed to disk before the media can be removed.

Companies that are reportedly considering this level of operating system support under their own versions of UNIX include NeXT, Inc. under Mach, and Hewlett-Packard Company (H-P) under HP-UX. H-P believes that the mitigation of the erase pass is crucial to the development of a high-performance rewritable optical file management system.

A Universal Logical Format for Rewritable Media

X3B11.1, the ANSI accredited committee for Optical Disk Volume and File Structure Standards, is working to create a logical file interchange standard for optical media, i.e., an optical file system[1]. Its immediate target is WORM media, but its work should be immediately extensible to rewritable media as well. Although virtually all rewritable implementations today support the native file system of the host computer, the removable optical media that they use cannot be read or written if under other operating systems without special software to interpret the "foreign" file system.

If a disk format encompassing the requirements of all major file system formats existed, such translation software would likely become widely available. The result of such a phenomenon would be a nearly universally usable, high-capacity, random access media. The potential ramifications of such a format are great indeed.

H-P is developing a product based on the X3B11.1 standard

that will incorporate the M-O performance enhancement described earlier, and has proposed use of this enhancement to the X3B11.1 committee.

Media Sector Size Issues

The ANSI/ISO standard for the physical characteristics of rewritable 5.25-inch optical media includes two variants of sector size: 512 and 1024 user bytes per sector. (Media sector size is determined at the time of its manufacture.) If both media types are to be accommodated, the possibility of two sector sizes presents a software integration issue for the following reasons:

- At most, only one of these sizes will match the sector size of an operating system's native file system.

- Media of a sector size other than that of the native file system may not be bootable.

The first issue is solved by proper buffering of data, but a performance problem exists for write operations if the file system sector size is smaller than that of the media being used. Writing a 512-byte sector to 1024-byte media requires that a 1024-byte sector be read, that it be merged with the 512 bytes to be written, and that the sector be erased (if M-O), the new sector data written, and the sector verified (if P-C). This write operation requires three passes over the media for both M-O and P-C media.

The second issue is of concern if a system's boot ROM code is tied to a fixed sector size for the boot device. Since 512 bytes is the base sector size for operating systems such as UNIX, MS-DOS, OS/2, DEC-VMS, and Apple Macintosh, the bootability of 1024-byte media on these systems is a potential problem. Some vendors have overcome this in SCSI host adapter firmware for MS-DOS and device driver software for the Macintosh by implementing a data merging algorithm for write operations (as just described) and a data extraction algorithm for reading, but it poses a problem for operating systems such as SunOS (Sun Microsystems' version of UNIX).

Removable Media Issues

The removability feature of optical media has been mentioned in a positive context herein, but it does pose a software development and integration challenge for the following reasons:

- A disk's file system must be in a quiescent state before the disk can be allowed to be removed.

- It must be possible to distinguish any one platter from all others.

- Media swapping such as that required by a multi-platter volume should be allowed.

The first point is only an issue if the host operating system buffers write data and may declare an operation complete before the media is actually written, as is the case with UNIX and other multitasking operating systems. This issue can probably be addressed through use of the SCSI PREVENT/ALLOW MEDIUM REMOVAL command to ensure that a piece of media can be considered fixed while its file system is dynamic.

The second point is of particular concern for installations that have data stored on a large set of disks that may often be swapped in and out of drives within an optical jukebox. Each disk surface must contain some unique ID in a label field in order for it to be correctly identified. Since most operating systems do not allow for such a field (or at least one that can virtually guarantee uniqueness), a special file or area on the disk must be set aside to retain this ID. The ID should be created and written only when the disk is first used, and could be constructed from the date, time, a serial number, a system drive number, and a random number.

The third point requires that a requested platter, such as one that is part of a multi-volume set, be made available when necessary. This requirement can be smoothly accommodated if media swapping is automated, i.e., a jukebox is available for this chore. However, manual swapping requires that an operator inserts a particular platter (whose identity can be verified by its unique ID field). Operating systems such as UNIX have no standard way to allow for such operator interaction because most flavors of UNIX have no concept of a removable medium.

Accommodating High-Capacity Media

The large data space on the surface of a rewritable optical disk (128MB to 500MB) has posed a problem for some operating systems that expected media to never surpass, for example, 32MB in size (as was the case for earlier versions of MS-DOS). Today, the latest versions of most popular software platforms have no problem in this regard. As a result, integrators should be aware of the minimum requirements for the environment in which their software can operate.

The SCSI Interface

As previously mentioned, virtually all rewritable optical drives are available with a SCSI interface. SCSI is popular for a number of reasons, including the fact that SCSI has been a standard feature on Apple Macintosh and Sun Microsystems' computers since around 1985. SCSI-based devices tend to be "plug-and-play" on such platforms, further encouraging SCSI's proliferation.

The SCSI INQUIRY command is used by a host to determine information about a device including its type, vendor ID, and revision level. Although the standard SCSI device type designation for rewritable optical drives is "optical memory device," most vendors have chosen to use "direct-access device." Since the latter is expected to be used by a magnetic disk, use of rewritable drives as if they were magnetic is more easily facilitated. Note, though, that accommodating any special rewritable media requirements (such as the technique described earlier in the "Mitigating Poor Performance" section) requires special handling by a device driver.

SCSI provides a generic set of commands for use by a wide variety of device types. Because of this, the integrator's job is simplified since special device considerations (such as defect management) are handled in the device itself. A device driver, however, is required for platforms lacking a standard SCSI port. Because there has been no standard protocol for setting up and issuing SCSI commands on such platforms, the SCSI standards committee organized an *ad hoc* group known as the SCSI-2 Common Access Method (CAM) Committee.

Although the CAM Committee has had some problems finalizing such a protocol, in mid-1990 Microsoft, Western Digital, Compaq, Adaptec, and NCR announced a layered device-driver architecture called LADDR which defines a protocol for OS/2. In addition, IBM finally endorsed SCSI with its introduction of two Micro Channel Architecture host adapters in April 1990.

The CAM Committee is now focused on defining a protocol for UNIX and Novell Netware.

Integrating Multifunction Optical Disk Drives

After much anticipation, multifunction optical disk drives that can read and write both W-O and rewritable media were first shown or announced by some vendors including Pioneer and Panasonic in mid-1990. The following three technology approaches are being used:

1. Write-once ablative and rewritable magneto-optical.
2. Write-once and rewritable, both using phase-change.
3. Write-once and rewritable, both using magneto-optical.

Unlike the other approaches, the first requires circuitry to handle two disparate technologies, increasing drive cost and the manufacturer's engineering effort. Panasonic P-C media for the second approach is identical for WORM and rewritable except for a difference in the optical sensing material and in media designators indicating WORM versus rewritable. H-P, which announced support for the third approach (W-O and rewritable using M-O) along with thirteen other drive, media, and computer vendors, uses identical M-O media, except for a code molded into the media indicating WORM versus rewritable.

Multifunction optical disk drives for all approaches have firmware that handles the media correctly, including disallowing sector overwrites on W-O media. Since the third approach uses M-O media even for W-O usage, the media is erased as the last step of the drive's SCSI FORMAT command.

Integrating a multifunction drive requires software to detect the current media type and ensure that all driver and applications software treat the media as W-O or rewritable. Hence, media type must be checked when the drive is first accessed and whenever there is a media change. Although the current media type can be determined from the Peripheral Device Type byte returned by the SCSI INQUIRY command, there is an important caveat regarding rewritable media in "The SCSI Interface" section of this chapter. Even though the drive itself will not allow sectors on W-O media to be overwritten, applications software that uses different algorithms based on the media type must be aware of the current media loaded. The integrator also must be aware of other ramifications of having to swap between media types while an application is up and running.

Interestingly, although the Pioneer/Laser Magnetic Storage Optical (LMSI)/Optimem drive (which uses the first approach) can sense the type of media loaded, it requires the device driver to determine the current type of media with the SCSI READ MODE command, and possibly allow for its use with the SCSI CHANGE MODE command. Both of these are vendor-unique commands that switch the drive circuitry between write-once and rewritable, including turning the M-O magnetic coil "on" or "off" as appropriate.

Conclusion

Rewritable optical disk drives are generally easy to integrate into today's computer systems because their logical operation is identical to that of today's widely available magnetic disk drives. However, issues regarding poor write performance, dual sector sizes, removability, and the availability of multifunction drives must be addressed by system integrators interested in creating versatile systems with good performance.

Its rewritability, removability, and high capacity have made rewritable optical media the best candidate for an interchangeable medium among disparate operating systems. When the ANSI X3B11.1 committee standardizes a generic file system for W-O and rewritable optical disk media, the necessary elements will be in place for universal interchangeability.

Note

1.   Brian Berg. "Optotech Systems Architecture (OSA): A File System Architecture for Removable Optical Media," *Optical Information Systems* Vol. 10, no. 2 (March/April, 1990): 84-89.

Directory of Organizations and Individuals

3M Company
420 North Bernardo Avenue
Mountain View, CA 94043
415.969.5200

3M Company
Optical Recording Department
Building 225-4S-09
St. Paul, MN 55144
800.328.1300
Rewritable optical disk media manufacturer. Offers rewritable disk capable of storing up to 650MB per disk side.

Absoft Corporation
2781 Bond Street
Rochester Hills, MI 48309
313.853.0050
FORTRAN 77 compiler is optimized to run on the NeXT workstation and allows porting programs written for the VAX/VMS, IBM/VS, Sun and Apollo machines to the NeXT. Supports version 0.9 of the NeXT operating system.

Accell Computer Corporation
17145 Bon
Karman Avenue, Suite 110
Irvine, CA 92714
714.757.1212
Offers rewritable optical storage subsystem for Macintosh users. Especially suited for computer-aided design, engineering and manufactur-

ing (CAD/CAM/CAE) multiple-image applications and can be used as a storage device in a LAN operating server system.

Advanced Decision System
1500 Plymouth Street
Mountain View, CA 94043
415.960.7300
Developing networking application of Jasmine's DirectOptical rewritable drive.

Advanced Graphic Applications, Inc. (AGA)
653 11th Avenue, 11th Floor
New York, NY 10036
212.265.0655
DISCUS (Data, Image, Sound, Communications Unified Storage) is available as a write-once and rewritable optical storage system for the IBM-PC and PS/2 and compatibles under OS/2 and DOS.

Offers DISCUS Rewritable jukebox for MS-DOS, OS/2 and SCO Xenix installations; it can store up to 56 M-O disk cartridges and offers approximately 35GB of online storage capacity.

Advanced Micro Devices
POB 3453
Mail Stop 59
Sunnyvale, CA 94088
408.732.2400

Alphatronix, Inc.
4900 Prospectus Drive, Suite 1000
POB 13687
Research Triangle Park, NC 27709
919.544.0001
Developed Inspire, a rewritable subsystem, for DEC, Sun and IBM-compatible computers based on the Sony rewritable drive. Offers a jukebox configuration for the Inspire subsystem for DEC and Sun workstations as well as AT-based PCs. Bypass is a software product that allows the user to use the same disk in a VAX and PC environment.

Rapidstore backs up files up to five times faster than 6250 BPI tape, operates as a normal VMS disk, initializes disk on-the-fly, defragments files, and supports wildcard operations for file and directory selection.

Ambertek Systems, Inc.
POB 7124
Thousand Oaks, CA 91359
805.493.1595
Marketing optical subsystems based on Sony's 12-inch WORM and rewritable optical drives for the IBM-PC and compatible systems; DEC VAX versions are under development.

American Color
2323 East Magnolia Street, Suite 118
Phoenix, AZ 85034
602.275.4347
Large color separation house used by the printing industry. American Color is using Sony's M-O drive for its image storage requirements. It specializes in the preparation of magazines, brochures, Sunday newspaper supplements and catalogs. It offers offset, flexography, and gravure printing processes.

American Digital Systems
490 Boston Post Road
Sudbury, MA 01776
508.443.7711
Offers the Masterdisk Optical, a rewritable optical storage subsystem which operates with all DEC, Q-bus, Unibus, 3100 series- and Bi-Bus-based systems.

American Image and Information Management (AIIM)
1101 Wayne Avenue, Suite 1100
Silver Spring, MD 20016
202.537.7716
Trade association. Sponsors annual conference; publishes series of monographs and *INFORM* magazine.

American National Standards Institute (ANSI)
Accredit Standards Committee X3
c/o Howard Kaikow
Digital Equipment Corporation
110 Spit Brook Road
Mail Stop KZ03-4/Z090
Nashua, NH
603.881.1122
X3B11.1 is responsible for developing optical disk volume and file

structure standards that will facilitate the interface of information on removable optical disks.

American National Standards Institute, Inc. (ANSI)
1430 Broadway
New York, NY 10018
212.642.4900
Organization associated with standards for all industries. Publishes the official SCSI standard specification. X3B11 is the standards committee involved with establishing optical media and drive standards. See ENDL Associates.

Apex Systems, Inc.
5785 Arapahoe Road, Suite D
Boulder, CO 80303
303.443.3393
Offers optical head/media testers for WORM and M-O rewritable media, as well as optical head characterization.

Applied Data Communications
14272 Chambers Road
Tustin, CA 92680-6998
714.731.9000
Offers a rewritable optical disk subsystem based on the Sony M-O drive. It supports Novell NetWare, Wang VS applications, and IBM-PC and compatibles. Expected future releases include H-P, NCR Tower, DEC PDP-11N, and Macintosh II applications.

Applied Magnetics Corporation
Optical Products Division
18960 Base Camp Road
Monument, CO 80132
303.488.2900
Signed an agreement with Hewlett-Packard to use certain H-P patents and expertise relating to M-O recording heads. Based on H-P's technology, the firm is now offering a 3.5-inch optic baseplate assembly which includes the optics module, linear actuator, focus and tracking actuator, and motor. Currently, Applied Magnetics Corporation is developing a line of optical recording heads and subassemblies which it will market to magnetic disk drive manufacturers.

Apunix, Inc.
9330 Carmel Mountain Road, Suite C
San Diego, CA 92129
800.827.8649
619.484.0074
Offers the Desktop Robotic Library which features a Ricoh rewritable optical disk drive and media in a 10-disk jukebox manufactured by International Data Engineering, Inc.

Artecon, Inc.
2440 Impala Drive
Box 9000, Department 5500
Carlsbad, CA 92008-0993
619.931.5500
Offers rewritable optical drive subsystem for Sun 3 Microsystems workstations. Systems integrator. Uses Sony M-O drive and runs on Sun OS 4.0.1 operating system with either Sun 3 or Sun 2 SCSI host adapter.

Asaca/Shibasoku
12509 Beatrice Street
Los Angeles, CA
213.827.7144
800.423.6347
Uses M-O disk to store up to 1600 frames of color still-store image data per 5.25-inch double-sided disk. The ADS-300 mainframe is also capable of controlling up to seven external dual-disk drives for a maximum online data bank of 11,200 frames.

Asahi Chemical Industry Company, Ltd.
Information Processing Systems Division
Department of Optical Disks
The Imperial Tower
1-1, 1-Chome, Uchisaiwai-cho
Chiyoda-ku
Tokyo 100, Japan
81.3.507.2463
Manufacturer of 5.25-inch M-O and WORM phase-change media.

Autometric
5301 Shawnee Road
Alexandria, VA 22312

703.658.4000
Using rewritable optical disk system to store complex Landsat satellite photographs of earth's surface.

Battelle Pacific Northwest Laboratories
Battelle Blvd.
Richland, WA 99352
509.375.3688
Developed rewritable optical recording and storage medium for which the patent was assigned to Optical Data, Inc.

Berg Software Design
P.O. Box 3488
Saratoga, CA 95070
408.741.5010
Consulting firm specializing in Unix and DOS device drivers and applications software for CD-ROM, WORM, and rewritable optical storage.

Brenco Computer Systems, Inc.
520 Fellowship Road, Suite 208
Mt. Laurel, NJ 08054
609.722.5600
Offers subsystem for IBM-PC/AT, PS/2, and compatible computers. Villanova University (Philadelphia, Pennsylvania) was one of the first end-users of a Brenco subsystem.

BusinessLand, Inc.
1001 Ridder Park Drive
San Jose, CA 95131
408.437.0400
The only retail computer store chain to offer the NeXT Computer.

Canon America, Inc.
One Canon Plaza
Lake Success, NY 10042-1113
516.488.6700
5.25-inch rewritable drive and media manufacturer. Investor in NeXT, Inc. and marketing NeXT computer in the Far East. Offering a desktop electronic filing system based on M-O technology. The Canonfile 250 offers a storage capacity of 256MB per disk side and incorporates an LCD, digital rotary scanner, keyboard, and laser printer.

Canon America markets its M-O disk drive as a complete subsystem for IBM-compatible and Macintosh. With 250MB of single-sided recording capacity, the M-O-5001S offers less than half the storage capacity of double-sided M-O disk systems manufactured by Maxtor, Ricoh, Sony, and other firms.

Canon, Ltd.
Information Systems
The Fleming Centre, United 1A
Fleming Way
Crawley, West Sussex
RH10 2MM United Kingdom
0293.561180
WORM and rewritable drive manufacturer; supplier of rewritable drive in the NeXT computer.

CAP International
One Longworth Circle
Norwell, MA 02061
617.982.9500
Market research and consulting.

Carlisle Memory Products
4001 West Airport Freeway
Bedford, TX 22091
Markets 5.25-inch WORM and rewritable disks as well as 3.5-inch rewritable disks manufactured by Daicel Chemical.

CBEMA (Computer and Business Equipment Manufacturers Association)
311 First Street, N.W.
Suite 500
Washington, D.C. 20001-2178
202.737.8888
Industry trade group administers the Approved Standards Committees (ASCs) which work on projects intended to become standards of ANSI.

Centel Federal Systems
11400 Commerce Park Drive
Reston, VA 22091
703.758.7000

Offers systems integration, connectivity, tempesting, security, network services for WORM, rewritable, and CD-ROM optical storage.

Chimera Systems
10540 Kinnard Avenue
Los Angeles, CA 90024
213.470.2998
Offers a 5.25-inch rewritable M-O optical disk subsystem for the Macintosh with an SCSI interface.

CIMTECH (National Centre for Information Media & Technology)
P.O. Box 109, College Lane
Hatfield, Herts
AL10 9AB United Kingdom
0707.279670
Publishers of the journal *Information Media and Technology*, sponsors conferences and seminars, and offers consulting in micrographics, videotex, CD-ROM, WORM, and rewritable optical storage as well as desktop publishing and word processing.

Cirrus Logic
1463 Center Point Drive
Mail Stop 81
Milpitas, CA 95035
408.945.8300

Cohasset Associates
505 North Lake Shore Drive
Chicago, IL 60611
312.527.1550
Publishers of *The Legality of Optical Storage* and sponsors of Optical Storage Laws and Regulations Conference.

Computer Peripherals Division
991 Knox Street
Torrance, CA 90502
213.515.3993
5.25-inch WORM and rewritable drive, and jukebox manufacturer.

Computer Upgrade Corporation
2901 East La Palma Avenue, Suite A

Anaheim, CA 92806
714.630.3457
Western U.S. Regional Distributor for Pioneer's multifunction
WORM/rewritable optical disk drive. Its Omnistor subsystem uses
the Pioneer multifunction drive. Offers line of rewritable optical disk
subsystems for DEC, IBM, and Sun computers.

Corel Systems Corporation
1600 Carling Avenue
Ottawa, Ontario, Canada K1Z 8R7
617.728.8200
Introduced interface kits for Maxoptix, Ricoh, and Sony 5.25-inch M-O
drives for Macintosh, IBM-PC and PS/2 environments. Kits include
Corel's own SCSI host adapter. Firm is developing rewritable optical
subsystem.

Corning Glass Works
Precision Molded Optics
Sullivan Park, WW-01-8
Corning, New York 14831
607.974.3495
Manufacturer of glass disk media substrates for rewritable and write-
once optical storage.

Cygnet Systems, Inc.
2560 Junction Avenue
San Jose, CA 95013
408.954.1800
Latest offering is a 5.25-inch rewritable optical jukebox, and the industry's first one-year comprehensive warranty for its full line of optical
disk jukeboxes. Offers a line of 12-inch and 5.25-inch WORM optical
jukeboxes. Jukebox Interface Management System (JIMS) is a software package.

Cygnet Systems, Inc.
10480 Little Patuxent Parkway
Suite 400
Columbia, MD 21044
301.740.8754

Daicel (USA), Inc.
611 West Sixth Street

Suite 2152
Los Angeles, CA 90017
213.629.3656
Write-once and rewritable optical disk media manufacturer: 12-, 8-,
5.25-, and 3.5-inch.

Dartmouth College
Language Resource Center
201 Bartlett Hall
Hanover, NH 03755
603.646.2624
Using Jasmine rewritable optical disk drive for backup and CD-ROM
test production.

Data Peripherals
Unit Four
Kenworthy Road
Astonfields Industrial Estate, Stafford
ST16 3DY United Kingdom
Offers rewritable optical subsystem based on Ricoh's RS-9200E 5.25-
inch M-O drive for IBM PC/AT and PS/2 environments. The subsys-
tem can be daisy-chained using its SCSI interface and is being market-
ed for CAD/CAM, desktop publishing, and graphics applications.

Data Systems Technology
585 Burbank, Suite A
Broomfield, CO 80020
303.466.5228
Offers custom optical controller development for 5.25-inch and 3.5-
inch rewritable and WORM storage drives.

Dateline Technology, Inc.
11811 N.E. First Street, Suite 307
Bellevue, WA 98005
800.548.5154
Offers a Sony 5.25-inch M-O drive with proprietary controller with a
built-in SCSI interface for use with Wang VS systems.

Decade Computers, Ltd.
Unity House
Kennetside, Newbury
Berks RG14 5PX United Kingdom

0635-38008
European distributor of the Alphatronix Inspire rewritable optical disk mass to rage system.

DEI
10170 Sorrento Valley Road
San Diego, CA 92121-1604
619.452.7840
Distributor of Daicel Chemical magneto-optic rewritable and WORM media in the U.S.

Delta Microsystems
5039 Preston Avenue
Livermore, CA 94550
415.449.6881
Offers a rewritable optical subsystem using Sony's 5.25-inch M-O drive for Sun's SPARC workstations and Sun's standard SCSI disk drive.

Dimensional Visions Group
718 Arch Street
Suite 202 North
Philadelphia, PA 19106
215.337.4686
Storing graphic images on Jasmine rewritable drive.

Disk/Trend Report
1925 Landings Drive
Mountain View, CA 94043
415.961.6209
Consulting, market research, and analyses. Co-sponsor of the annual international Data Storage Conference which includes coverage of optical rewritable storage markets and technology.

Distributed Logic Corporation (Dilog)
1555 South Sinclair Street
Anaheim, CA 92806
714.937.5700
Offers a rewritable optical storage subsystem for DEC Q-Bus and Unibus users and SCSI interface.

Dolphin Systems Technology
1701 East Edinger Avenue

Building G
Santa Ana, CA 92705
714.558.3220
Sonar 600 rewritable optical subsystem for Macintosh, Sun, and IBM-PC microcomputers. Stand-alone unit uses Sony M-O drive.

E. I. DuPont Nemours, Inc.
Imaging Systems Department
Eagle Run
POB 6099
Newark, DE 19702
302.733.9455
FastTrax is an engineering drawing and related-documents management system that integrates a scanner, rewritable and WORM drive, and hard disk. It is a computerized graphic database that creates a bit-mapped (faster) representation of engineering, architectural, and other types of drawings. It stores associated documents and textual information related to drawings. Opti-Safe is an optical archival system for the printing and graphic arts industry.

DynaTek Automation Systems, Inc.
1515 Tangiers Road
Toronto, Canada M3J 2B1
416.636.3000
Integrated LMSI/Pioneer/Optimem sampled servo 5.25-inch multi-function optical disk drive into DOS, Macintosh, Novell, DEC, Unix/Xenix, Sun, and PS/2 environments.

Electronic Data Systems Corporation
7171 Forest Lane
Dallas, TX 75230
214.661.6188
Systems integrator in banking/financial, federal government, insurance, health care, manufacturing, retail, state and local governments, transportation, utilities, international communications, and wholesale/distribution markets.

Electronic Data Systems Corporation
Demand Services Division
13600 EDS Drive
Herndon, VA 22071
703.742.2000

Systems integrator. Offers an Integrated Document Processing (IDP) service, a vendor-independent rewritable and WORM-based approach for capturing, storing, retrieving and publishing data that provides an open architecture solution for Unix, VMS, DOS, and OS/2-based systems.

Electronic Trend Publications
12930 Saratoga Avenue, Suite D1
Saratoga, CA 95070
408.996.7416
Market research and analyses. *The Impact of Optical Technology on Paper, Microform and Magnetic Disk and Tape Storage* is a market research report.

ENDL Associates
29112 Country Hills Road
San Juan Capistrano, CA 92675
714.364.9626
Consulting organization owned by Ken Hallam, who chairs the ANSI Technical Comittee on Optical Media standardization, X3B11.

ENDL Publications
14426 Black Walnut Court
Saratoga, CA 95070
408.867.6630
Publishes the *ENDL Letter*. Owned by Dal Allan, who vice chairs the ANSI Technological Committee on SCSI and EDSI, X 3T9.2.

Energy Conversion Devices
1675 West Maple Road
Troy, MI 48084
313.280.1900
Developer of phase-change rewritable technology based on the structural rearrangement of a thin film of material that stores information in a pattern of microscopic dots created by a laser. Technology being used by Matsushita.

Epson America, Inc.
3145 Kashiwa Street
Torrance, CA 90505

Frame Technology Corporation
2911 Zanker Road
San Jose, CA 94134
408.433.3311
Uses the NeXT computer with Display PostScript.

Freeman Associates, Inc.
311 East Carrillo Street
Santa Barbara, CA 93101

Fuji Photo Film Co., Ltd.
Optical Memory Project
26-30, Nishiazabu 2-chome
Minato-ku, Tokyo 106, Japan
81.3.406.2492
Developed 5.25-inch optical products including ablative and dye-polymer WORM as well as M-O rewritable media. Intends to introduce 3.5-inch M-O media compatible with Maxoptix and Sony 3.5-inch M-O drives.

FWB, Inc.
2040 Polk Street, Suite 215
San Francisco, CA 94109
415.474.8055
Offers the hammerDisk600, a rewritable optical subsystem for Apple Macintosh network users for online backup data archiving applications. Uses the Ricoh 5.25-inch M-O rewritable drive.

Glaxo, Inc.
5 Moore Drive
Research Triangle Park, NC 27709
919.248.2100
Installed Alphatronix rewritable system to store physiologic data.

GoldStar
1130 East Arques Avenue
Sunnyvale, CA 94086
408.737.8575
Offers WORM as well as phase-change and rewritable 5.25-inch drives.

Gorham Advanced Materials Institute
POB 250
Gorham, ME 04038
207.892.5445
Thin Films for Electronic Optoelectronic and Optical Applications: Market Forecasts, Technology Assessments and New Business Opportunities to 1992 is a multi-client study.

Grenat Logiciel
6, Avenue des Andes, Bt. 4
Mini-Park, Z.I. Courtaboeuf,
91952 Les Ulis Cedex, France
33.1.64.46.45.54
STARFILE is a file management package for WORM disks and works on Sun, IBM-PC/XT/AT, VAX, Prime, Norsk Data, VMS, Macintosh and Unix-based machines. STARFILE Rewritable is based on the same principles as rewritable drives. Selected by European Space Agency for optical archiving of data from ERS 1 satellite.

GTX
8836 North 23rd Avenue
Phoenix, AZ
602.870.1696
Supplier of drawing conversion and management systems. The Drawing Management System incorporates LAN, mass storage devices, expert system techniques, raster and CAD vector processing. Engineering drawing system based on GTX 5000 raster to vector workstation using Shugart or Optimem WORM drives. Also offers rewritable system.

GTX, Ltd.
Farley Hall
London Road, Binfield
Bracknell, Berks RG12 5EU United Kingdom

Herstal Automation
3171 West Twelve Mile Road
Berkeley, MI 48072
313.548.2001
Developing optical subsystems based on Hewlett-Packard 1000, 3000, 9000 series Unix workstations. These subsystems will feature Maxtor WORM and Ricoh rewritable 5.25-inch drives.

Hewlett-Packard Company
3404 East Harmony Road
Fort Collins, CO 80525-9599
303.857.1501

Hewlett-Packard Company
Greeley Storage Division
700 71st Avenue
Greeley, CO 80634
303.350.4580
Offers one 5.25-inch multifunction optical disk drive (C1716M) using continuous composite servo format M-O media for both M-O and write-once functions based on Sony technology. Also offers a version of Advanced Image Management System using multifunction optical drives. The Series 9000 Model 800 runs Plexus Software and Calera's OCR technology.

Acquired the assets of Optotech, Inc., developer of a 5.25-inch rewritable drive that reportedly works with media from Sony, PDO, Fuji Photo Film, Canon, 3M and others. Optotech sold H-P all inventory and necessary materials to manufacture the drives. Assets included engineering contracts, drawings, equipment, supplier lists, technology patents, and leases for buildings.

The HP C171QA is an Optical Disk Library System, a rewritable optical disk autochanger using the Sony SM-O-D501 5.25-inch rewritable drive and the SM-O-C501, a SCSI host controller board. The HP Series 6300 Model 200GBA library stores up to 20.8GB of data on 32 5.25-inch disks and uses the SCSI interface.

Hewlett-Packard Company
3000 Hanover Street
Palo Alto, CA 94304
415.857.1501
Research and development laboratory.

Hewlett-Packard Company
Peripherals Group
16399 West Bernardo Drive
San Diego, CA 92127-1899
619.487.4100

Hewlett-Packard U.K., Ltd.
Pinewood Information Systems Division

Nine Mile Ride
Wokingham, Berkshire
RG11 3LL United Kingdom
44.344.763507
Announced the Advanced Image Management System (AIMS), a Unix-based document imaging platform to be marketed through VAR network. Uses software from Plexus and H-P's 5.25-inch jukebox with Sony M-O drives for image storage.

Hi-Tech Business Corporation
9460 Wilshire Blvd., Suite 514
Beverley Hills, CA
213.276.9361
Developing rewritable optical media based on magnetic bubble technology. The technology uses lasers to detect magnetic bubbles in multiple, micro-thin layers of transparent media which allows data to be stored in both vertical and horizontal planes thus greatly increasing storage density.

Hitachi America Ltd.
Computer Division
Hitachi Plaza
2000 Sierra Point Parkway
Brisbane, CA 9400
415.872.1902
Manufacturer of 5.25-inch rewritable optical disk drive, the OF112S SCSI formatter/controller, and WORM 12-inch drive and jukebox manufacturer.

Hitachi Sales Corporation
East Coast Office
Natick, MA 01760-1506
617.655.5501
Regional office.

Hitachi-Maxell
12880 Moore Street
Cerritos, CA 90701
213.926.0916
WORM, rewritable, and read-only optical media manufacturer.

Hoechst Celanese Corporation
Technology Development Optical Disk
One Main Street
Chatham, NJ 07928
201.635.4228
Ozadisc is the firm's 3.5- and 5.25-inch magneto-optic rewritable disk media and 5.25-inch dye-polymer WORM media. Joint venture with Nakamichi and KerDix to produce magneto-optic rewritable optical disks.

Hoechst Aktiengesellschaft
D-6230 Frankfurt 80
Federal Republic of Germany
49.069.305.3737
A member of a European consortium developing M-O drives, the firm has received funding and approval for the ESPRIT-Project 2013 which is intended to improve M-O technology. Hoechst is working with Lexikon, a subsidiary of Olivetti in Italy, Sagem, a French electronic firm, Coventry Polytechnic in the U.K., and the Research Institutes CEA-Division IETI in France.

IBM Corporation
9000 South Rita Road
Building 030-75W
Tucson, AZ 85744

Idemitsu Petrochemical PMPD
1-1 Marunouchi 3-chome, Chiyoda-ku
Tokyo 100, Japan

Idemitsu Petrochemical PMPD
50 Rockefeller Plaza, Suite 103B
New York, NY 10020

Image Business Systems Corporation
Two Grand Central Tower
New York, NY 10017
212.972.4400
800.YES.4.IBS
Spin-off of International Systems Services Company's document imaging business. Specializes in the integration of image processing into information systems. ImageSystem is a LAN-based document han-

dling imaging application that runs on the IBM RT system under AIX. Signed cooperative marketing agreement with IBM which now owns a minority equity in the firm. Offers WORM and rewritable versions of ImageSystem, an optional Cygnet jukebox.

Institute for Computer Sciences & Technology
National Bureau of Standards
Technology Building, Room A61
Gaithersburg, MD
301.975.2947
Active in establishing optical disk standards including media testing.

International Data Corporation (IDC)
Integrated Business Systems Services
5 Speen Street
Framingham, MA 01701
508.872.8200
"Integrated Business Systems: Integrated Office Systems and Document Management" is an IDC Market Planning Service. Publishes market research studies and analyses.

International Disk Equipment and Materials Association (IDEMA)
710 Lakeway, Suite 170
Sunnyvale, CA 94086
408.720.9352
A trade association serving suppliers of components for both magnetic and optical disk drives.

International Information Management Congress (IMC)
345 Woodcliff Drive
Fairport, NY 14450
716.383.8330
The IMC is the international trade association for the document imaging industry. Distributes document management technologies through journals, exhibitions, and conferences.

Iomega Coporation
1821 West 4000 South
Roy, UT 84067
801.778.1000
Offers M-O drive-based subsystems for Unix, NetWare 286 and OS/2 environments.

Jasmine
1740 Army Street
San Francisco, CA 94124
415.282.1111
DirectOptical is a 5.25-inch rewritable optical subsystem, based on the Ricoh engine and integrated with a Macintosh.

Kode
Division of Odetics, Inc.
1515 South Manchester
Anaheim, CA 92802-2907
714.758.0400
Time Interval Analyzers for measuring and testing bit shift and jitter in optical disk drives. Used by Cherokee, Eastman Kodak, Daicel, DEC, IBM, Maxtor, Optical Data, Panasonic, PDO, Sony, Verbatim, and others.

Kubota, Ltd.
Osaka, Japan
Entered into a joint venture with Maxtor to form Maxoptix Corporation based in San Jose, CA. Under this five-year agreement, Kubota will spend twelve million dollars for a twenty-five percent equity share and obtain worldwide manufacturer rights and exclusive marketing rights.

Kuraray Plasmon Data Systems Company
4-Ageba-cho
Shinjuku-ku
Tokyo 162, Japan
81.3.277.3320

Kuraray Company, Ltd.
M-O Disk Promotion Department
Shin-Nihonbashi Building
3-8-2, Nihonbashi, Chou-ku
Tokyo 103, Japan
81.3.277.3363

Laser Magnetic Storage International Company (LMSI)
4425 ArrowsWest Drive
Colorado Springs, CO 80907
303.593.4214

Optical disk drive manufacturer; supports Pioneer SS multifunction drive format.

LightStore Company
1825 South Grant Street, Suite 550
San Mateo, CA 94402
415.572.2333
A subsidiary of Mitsui Petrochemical, this company has developed a 5.25-inch rewritable optical drive with a disk that is available with either 512 or 1024 sectors.

Linotype
425 Oser Avenue
Hauppauge, NY 11788
516.434.2000
OEM for Jasmine drive. Intends to market subsystem to publishing industry.

Literal Corporation (formerly Laserdrive Ltd. and ISi)
2768 Janitell Road
Colorado Springs, CO 80906
303.579.0460
Eastman Kodak and Olivetti purchased eighty percent of the company in 1989. Literal has absorbed Verbatim's 5.25- and 3.25-inch TMO rewritable optical drive and system development. Expects to manufacture 3.5-inch M-O drives in California, and both 5.25-inch WORM and rewritable 5.25-inch multifunction drives using phase-change media. Offers three 5.25-inch WORM drives for Apple Computer's Macintosh II (Model 820), IBM-compatibles, and Digital Equipment Corporation's Micro. Purchased ISi (Colorado Springs, CO).

MACsetra Technologies International, Inc.
2237 York Avenue
Saskatoon, Saskatchewan
Canada AJ7 1H0
306.955.0022
The Genesis G6000 is a rewritable optical subsystem featuring Ricoh M-O rewritable drives and the Macintosh family of microcomputers including the IIcx, IIx, and SE/30.

Mass Optical Storage Technology, Inc. (MOST)
11205 Knot Avenue, Suite B

Cypress, CA 90630
714.898.9400
Developing a 3.5-inch M-O rewritable drive. MOST is funded through
Nakamichi and has completed an engineering prototype.

Matsushita Electric Industrial Company
1006 Kadoma
Kadoma City
Osaka 571 Japan
06.908.1121
Commercialized rewritable 3.5-inch 280MB optical disk in Japan using
phase-change optical media. Firm offers optical storage system designed for high-definition, digitally encoded images and uses 12-inch
WORM phase-change disks.

Maxcess, Inc.
314 North 13th Street, Suite 806
Philadelphia, PA 19108
215.928.1213
Offers 600L rewritable optical disk subsystem (using Sony M-O drive)
for Macintosh.

Maxell Corporation
12880 Moore Street
Cerritos, CA 90701
213.926.0926
Offers WORM and rewritable (M-O) optical disk media and cartridges. The rewritable cartridges are designed for use in Hitachi's 5.25-
inch rewritable optical drives.

Maxoptix Corporation
150 River Oaks
San Jose, CA 95134
408.432.1700
Joint venture of Maxtor and Kubota Ltd. Maxtor transferred the technology and personnel for rewritable and WORM optical disk products
to this joint venture. Focus on Tahiti 1, a 5.25-inch rewritable drive developed by Maxtor.

Maxtor Corporation
150 River Oaks Parkway
San Jose, CA 95134

408.432.1700
Discontinued Fiji 1, a 3.5-inch rewritable optical drive. Acquired systems integrator Storage Dimensions. The Tahiti 1, a 5.25-inch 1GB drive, has been repeatedly delayed. It claims a 35ms access time and thus is expected to serve as a primary storage device, replacing or complementing a hard disk drive.

Meckler Corporation
11 Ferry Lane West
Westport, CT 06880
203.226.6967
Publishes bi-monthly *Document Image Automation* (formerly *Optical Information Systems*) which contains in-depth articles and monthly *DIA Update* which focuses on current news about write-once and rewritable optical disk technology and application developments. Sponsors annual DIA (Document Image Automation) conference.

Meckler, Ltd.
247-249 Vauxhall Bridge Rd.
London SW1V 1HQ
01.931.9985

Micro Design International, Inc.
6985 University Blvd.
Winter Park, FL 32792
407.677.8333
The LaserBank 600 R is a rewritable optical disk subsystem with software interfaces for MS-DOS, SCO XENIX or Novell NetWare operating systems. Subsystem uses Sony M-O drive. Offers a variety of software interfaces including the XENIX mountable and the LaserBank transparent.

Micro Dynamics, Ltd.
8555 Sixteenth Street, Suite 802
Silver Spring, MD 20910
301.589.6300
MARS is a Multi-user Archival Retrieval System that integrates the Calera Recognition System, Macintosh II, high-speed scanner, LAN, and ISI's 5.25-inch WORM drive. LSMI's and Sony's 12-inch WORM

drives are optional. New upgrades include jukeboxes, rewritable optical storage, and LAN software.

MicroNet Technology
20 Mason
Irvine, CA 92718
714.837.6033
Offers Sony M-O disk subsystem for IBM-PC/AT, PS/2 and compatible computers. When configured with a special device driver, the Micro/Optical system can "splice" two drives into one logical volume, giving customers access to 600MB of rewritable optical storage without having to turn over the disk.

Microtech International
158 Commerce Street
East Haven, CT 06512
203.468.6223
Offers OR650 rewritable optical storage system for Macintosh using Sony M-O drive.

Mitsubishi Electronics America, Inc.
Computer Peripherals Division
991 Knox Street
Torrance, CA 90502
213.515.3993
5.25-inch WORM and rewritable drive and jukebox manufacturer.

Mitsubishi Kasei
5-2 Marunouchi 2-Chome
Chiyoda-Ku, Tokyo, Japan
81.03.282.6760
Offers 5.25-inch WORM and 3.5- and 5.25-inch M-O rewritable optical media.

Mitsubishi Kasei America
81 Main Street, Suite 401
White Plains, NY 10601
914.761.9450
Demonstrated 5.25- and 3.5-inch M-O disks. Media qualifies for drives manufactured by Mitsubishi Electronics and has been demonstrated with Ricoh drive.

Mitsui Petrochemical Industries, Ltd.
c/o **Lightstore Company**
1825 South Grant Street, Suite 550
San Mateo, CA 94402
415.572.2333

Mitsui Petrochemical Industries
Memory Devices Department
Kasumigaseki Building
P.O. Box 90
3-2-5 Kasumigaseki , Chiyoda-ku
Tokyo 100, Japan
81.3.580.1646

National Institute of Standards and Technology (NIST)
Building 225-A61
Gaithersburg, MD 20899
301.975.2947
Sponsors Optical Media Research program for media testing and standardization.

New Logic Research
1552 Beach Street
Oakland, CA
415.655.7305
Startup company developing polymer-dye rewritable media.

New York Life Insurance Company
51 Madison Avenue
New York, NY 1101
212.576.7778
End-user of AGA's WORM-based DISCUS. The information systems division is evaluating the NeXT Computer.

Next Technology Corporation, Ltd.
St. Johns Innovation Centre
Cambridge CB4 4WS United Kingdom
44.223.421.180
Voyager is a jukebox capable of storing up to 180 5.25-inch rewritable disks.

NeXT, Inc.
3475 Deer Creek Road
Palo Alto, CA 94304
415.424.8500
Manufacturer of the NeXT workstation which uses the Canon rewritable optical drive as its primary storage device. Offers NeXT lower-cost network user system that omits the M-O disk drive used in original workstation. All NeXT users have received a 40MB Quadram hard disk drive free of charge.

Software developers include Frame Technology and Lotus. The latter reportedly plans to develop an advanced version of Lotus 1-2-3 for NeXT's rewritable optical drive.

Nissei Sangyo America, Ltd.
460 East Middlefield Road
Mountain View, CA 94043
415.969.1100
Handles U.S. sales and marketing for Asahi Chemical, manufacturer of M-O and phase-change media.

Nixdorf Computer AG
Product Division Open Systems
D-4790 Paderborn
Federal Republic of Germany
49.5251.10.3666

Nixdorf Computer AG
300 Third Avenue
Waltham, MA 02154
617.890.3600

NKK
Peripheral Device Department
Electronics Division
Hieikudankita Building
4-1-3 Kudankita
Chiyoda-ku
Tokyo 102, Japan
81.03.288.3840

NKK offers two versions of a 56-disk cartridge 5.25-inch Disc Inn juke-box: one based on the Pioneer multifunction drive, and the other on the Sony multifunction device.

North American Philips
100 East 42nd Street
New York, NY 10017
212.697.3600

Ocean Microsystems, Inc.
246 East Hacienda Avenue
Campbell, CA 95008
800.262.3261
408.374.8300
Has demonstrated the Vista 130, a 3.5-inch rewritable optical drive developed by Mass Optical Storage Technologies (MOST). Ocean and MOST are subsidiaries of Nakamichi. Ocean is developing software for a variety of microcomputers and workstations include Apple, IBM, and Sun. Also offers 9650R Tidelwave subsystem using Sony M-O drive.

Olympus Corporation
Special Products Division
3000 Marcus Avenue, Suite 1E7
Lake Success, NY
516.488.3880
Developed rewritable optical disk SCSI subsystem.

Olympus Corporation
Technology Development Center
23456 Hawthorne Blvd., Suite 120
Torrance, CA 90505
213.373.0696
MD-D501E is a 5.25-inch magneto-optical rewritable drive that uses 3M media. Developed an SCSI-based subsystem.

Olympus Optical Company GmbH
Wendenstrasse 14-16
D-2000 Hamburg 1

Federal Republic of Germany
49402.377.3168
Model ME-S5010E is a standalone 5.25-inch magneto-optic rewritable
drive; the Model ME-D5010E is a built-in unit.

Olympus Optical Co., Ltd.
Planning and Sales Section
Optical Memory Division
San-ei Building
22-2, Nishi-Shinjuki
1-chome, Shinjuku-ku
Tokyo, Japan
81.3.340.2270

Optex Corporation
2 Research Court
Rockville, MD 20850
301.840.0011
Demonstrated that its Electron Trapping Optical Memory (ETOM)
disk completed a 100 million read, write and erase cycle test without
any material degradation or change in the physical characteristics of
the media. The drive design was developed by Vision Three.

Optical Access International
36 Commerce Way
Woburn, MA 01801
617.935.2679
Signed a marketing agreement with Pioneer to sell its multifunction
and WORM subsystems to the Macintosh market.

Optical Data, Inc. (ODI)
9400 S.W. Gemini Drive
Beaverton, OR 97005
503.626.2211
Shut down in early 1990 after Tandy's announcement that it would introduce a commercial version of ODI's flexible rewritable optical media in its THOR-CD product line. Teijin, Ltd. is actively developing
ODI's technology under license and expects to introduce commercial
products. Developer of optical media including a flexible rewritable
optical media.

Optical Storage Corporation
Akasaka Twin Tower (East)
16th Floor
2-17-22, Akasaka
Minato-ku, Tokyo 107, Japan
81.3.583.3263

Optimage, Inc.
POB 44
Adelaide Postal Station
Toronto M5C 2H8 Canada
This system integrator intends to offer rewritable drive for use in its
PC-based image and document storage and retrieval system.

Optimem
297 North Bernardo Avenue
Mountain View, CA 94304
415.961.1800

Optimem
Eastern Region
167 Flanders Street
Rochester, NY 14619
716.436.0150

Optimem
Midwest Region
6034 West Courtyard Drive
Third Floor, Suite 305
Austin, TX 78730
512.338.2118

Optimem
Federal Division
1850 Centennial Park Drive
Suite 300
Reston, VA 22091
703.648.1568

Optimem
Cipher House
Ashville Way

Wokingham, Berkshire
RG11 2PL United Kingdom
44.0734.775757

Optotech, Inc.
740 Wooten Road
Colorado Springs, CO 80915
303.570.7500
Key assets of Optotech were acquired by Hewlett-Packard at the end of 1989. Although H-P acquired the majority of Optotech's assets, Optotech will continue to exist as a separate entity.

Panasonic Industrial Company
Memory Systems Division
1600 McCandless Drive
Milpitas, CA 95035
408.262.2200
The Model LF-9000S is a 5.25-inch M-O drive.

Panasonic
One Panasonic Way
Secaucus, NJ 07094
201.348.7777

Pegasus Disk Technologies
55 Crest Avenue
Walnut Creek, CA 94595
415.938.3345
415.439.7845
WORM and rewritable optical drive and jukebox integration firm. Specializes in Sony network compatible jukeboxes.

Pentax Teknologies
880 Interlocken Parkway
Broomfield, CO 80020
303.460.1600
Manufacturer of 5.25-inch WORM and magneto-optic heads. The Optical Head and Media Tester can be used for WORM, CD, LaserVision, and M-O rewritable drives.

Perceptive Solutions, Inc.
1509 Falcom, Suite 104

DeSoto, TX 75115
214.224.6774
Offers the hyperSTORE, a one-controller solution to applications that
utilize a variety of mass storage devices including rewritable optical
disk drives and floppies.

Peripheral Land, Inc.
47421 Bayside Parkway
Fremont, CA 94538
415.657.2211
Offers Infinity Optical rewritable storage subsystem for IBM-PC/AT/
XT and PS/2 computers as well as Macintosh using Sony M-O drive.
Comes in single- or double-drive configurations and bundled with an
extensive collection of utility software: TurboBack, TurboCache, Tur-
boOptizimer, and ACE! from Casady and Green, Inc., a security software package for the Macintosh.

Philips and Du Pont Optical
1409 Foulk Road
Wilmington, DE 19803
302.479.2507
Offers 12-inch and 5.25-inch magneto-optic (M-O) rewritable optical
disk media which will be used with Maxtor's Tahiti 1 drive. Manufactures rewritable optical disks at its Kings Mountain, North Carolina
plant.

Philips Business Systems
Elektra House
Bergholt Road
Colchester
Essex CO4 5BE United Kingdom
0206-575115
Drive and media manufacturer.

Philips Research Laboratories
Building WY 7
5600 JA Eindhoven
The Netherlands
31.40.742424
Reported promising group of rewritable optical materials such as gal-
lium antimonide and indium antimonide using phase change tech-

niques for the recording of analog and digital signals. Materials will not be used in new products in the near term.

Pinnacle Micro
15265 Alton Parkway
Irvine, CA 92718
800.553.7070
714.727.3300
Implementation of the Sony M-O drive, the SM-O-S501, in a Macintosh computer environment. The REO-650 is a single drive, SCSI system; the REO-1300 is a dual-drive subsystem. Software supports a host of working environments: Unix, Xenix, Novell and NetWare 2.1.

Engineered a Macintosh-compatible 16GB rewritable optical disk jukebox (REO-16000) which is being distributed by Ingram Micro D Inc.

Pioneer Communications of America
600 East Crescent Avenue
Upper Saddle River, NJ 07458
201.327.6400
Announced a 5.25-inch multifunction optical disk drive that can read and write both M-O rewritable media and dye-polymer WORM media.

Also announced a prototype M-O videodisc recorder/player that uses M-O technology to store video in analog format. Developed jointly with KDD, Pioneer expects to offer this rewritable M-O videodisc system to the broadcasting industry.

NKK offers a 56-disk cartridge 5.25-inch Disc Inn jukebox based on the Pioneer multifunction drive.

Pioneer Electronic Corporation
Industrial Systems Division
4-1, Meguro 1-Chome
Meguro-ku, Tokyo 153 Japan

Pioneer Electronics Corporation
OMDD ENgineering Department
2610 Honazono 4-Chome
Tokorotawa-shi Saitama 359 Japan

Pioneer Laser Technology
Branch Office

106, Field Way
Greenford, Middlesex
UB6 8UZ United Kingdom
01.575.5757

Pioneer Electronic (Europe) N.V.
Headquarters Office
Keelberglaan 1
2740 Beveran, Belgium
03.750.0511

Pioneer Electronics Australia, PTY, Ltd.
178-184 Boundary Road
Braeside, Victoria 3195, Australia
03.580.9911

RACET Computes, Ltd.
3150 East Birch Street
Brea, CA 92621
714.579.1725
The COSM-OS 600 M-O is a standalone rewritable optical subsystem compatible with IBM compatibles and Macintosh and uses Sony M-O drive.

Reflection Systems, Inc.
West Tasman Street
San Jose, CA
Offers an 11GB multifunction optical jukebox.

Relax Technology
3101 Whipple Road, Suite 22
Union City, CA 94587
415.471.6112
Offers rewritable optical disk subsystem using Ricoh M-O drive for Macintosh, Sun or IBM-PCs.

Remark Associates
431 Clipper Street
San Francisco, CA 94114
415.641.6033

Principal is Les Cowan. Consulting firm devoted to the development and utilization of optical storage technologies.

Ricoh Corporation
Tenkoh 50 Building
Mfg. Department No. 2
2-7-19 Shin-Yokohama, Kohoku-ku
Components Division
Tokyo, 222 Japan
81.45.474.7375

Ricoh Corporation
5150 El Camino Real, Suite D-20
Los Altos, CA 94022
415.962.0443
WORM and rewritable optical disk drive manufacturer. The RO-5030E is a 5.25-inch rewritable optical drive and was jointly developed with Olympus Corporation. Offers an enhanced version of its rewritable disk drive that supports latest ISO standards.

Ricoh Deutschland GmbH
Data Processing Section
Mergenthaler Allee 38-40
6236 Eschborn 1
Federal Republic of Germany
0.6196.906.0

Ricoh Europe
Dusseldorf Branch
Hansaalle 201
4000 Dusseldorf 11
Federal Republic of Germany
49.0.211.5285.0

Ricoh UK, Ltd.
Ricoh House
2 Plane Tree Crescent
Feltham, Middlesex
TW13 7HG United Kingdom
01.751.6611

Rothchild Consultants
256 Laguna Honda Blvd.
San Francisco, CA 94116-1496
415.681.3700
Optical memory marketing and technology consulting services offered worldwide. Publications include *Optical Memory News* and the *Optical Memory Report*. The firm offers a continuing information service, Optical System Information Service, and sponsors the Technology Opportunity Conferences.

Russell Industries
884 Tourmaline Drive
Newbury Park, CA 91320
805.499.6789
Marketing Kuraray's 5.25-inch "Lifetime" M-O media, a second source for Sony M-O drives.

Seiko Epson Corporation
OEM Project Suwaminami Branch
1010 Fijimi Fijimi-machi, Suwa-gun
Nagano-ken, 399-02 Japan
81.266.62.6020

Seiko Epson, Ltd.
Epson America
OEM Division
3415 Kashiwa Street
Torrance, CA 90505
213.534.4500

Semi-Tech Microelectronics
131 McNabb Street
Markham, Ontario
L3R 5V7 Canada
Developing a low-end 5.25-inch M-O rewritable optical drive and media.

Sharp/SDI
16841 Armstrong Avenue
Irvine, CA 92714-4979

Sharp Electronics Corporation
10 Sharp Plaza

Mahway, NJ 07430-2135
201.529.8200
201.529.8970
Model JY-500 is an ISO-compatible 5.25-inch rewritable magneto-optic drive and media. The firm has demonstrated a computer color imaging system that uses a color scanner, color thermal transfer printer, and Model JY-500.

SKC Limited
Chonan, South Korea
Developing M-O media.

Software Architects
Totem Triangle Center
4327 Rucker Avenue
Everett, WA 98203
206.252.6897
Offers FormatterOne SCSI Driver & Utility which facilitates the installation of Canon, Ricoh, and Sony rewritable optical disk drives on the Macintosh.

Sony Corporation of America
Optical Storage Technology
Sony Drive
Park Ridge, NJ 07656
201.930.6025
Offers 5.25-inch M-O ISO standard rewritable drive and media.
      NKK offers a 56-disk cartridge 5.25-inch Disc Inn jukebox based on the Sony multifunction drive.

Sony Corporation
M-O Business Development Division
Storage Systems Group
Atsugi Technology Center #2
2255 Okata, Atsugi City
Kanagawa 243, Japan
81.462.27.2182

Sony Corporation
1-7-4 Konan, Minato-ku
Tokyo 108, Japan

Sony Corporation
4-10-18 Takanawa, Minato-ku
Tokyo 108 Japan
Demonstrated a 3.5-inch M-O disk (CD-M-O) as well as a 12-inch re-writable M-O videodisc that can record 24 minutes of video per side in Japan.

Sony Corporation
Magnetic Products Europe
Sony Europa GmbH
Hugo-Eckener-Strabe 20
D-5000 Cologne 30,
Federal Republic of Germany
(0221.) 5966.226

Sony Corporation
Data Media Sales Division
Magnetic Products Group
6-7-35, Kitashinagawa 6-chome
Shinagawa-ku
Tokyo, 141 Japan
03. 338.3185

Sony Microsystems Company
1049 Elwell Court
Palo Alto, CA 94303
415.965.4492
Offers high-performance workstations that can be configured with re-writable optical storage.

SPIE (International Society for Optical Engineers)
POB 10
Bellingham, WA 98227-0010
206.676.3290
Professional organization that publishes *Optical Engineering* journal and *Optical Engineering Reports*. SPIE also sponsors conferences.

Storage Dimensions
2145 Hamilton Avenue
San Jose, CA 95125
408.879.0300

Subsidiary of Maxtor Corporation. The firm has demonstrated the Tahiti 1 rewritable drive with an IBM-PC/AT. LaserStor is a 5.25-inch optical subsystem for IBM-PC, IBM PS/2, and Macintosh environments with Ricoh/Maxtor WORM and rewritable drives. LaserCache is a software package. Storage Dimensions owns the rights to Tallgrass Technologies LightFile product line.

StoragePlus, Inc. (formerly Sumo Systems)
1580 Old Oakland Road
Suite C-103
San Jose, CA 95131
408.286.5744
Markets a rewritable optical subsystem, the RSSM600-C series, using the Ricoh M-O rewritable drive for the Macintosh. The firm also supplies a host adapter for the IBM-PC and compatibles.

Summus Computer Systems
17171 Park Row, Suite 300
Houston, TX 77084
713.578.3303
Offers LightDisk 650 rewritable subsystem for Macintosh, DEC and Q-Bus and Unibus computers, Sun workstations and IBM-PC/AT and compatibles using Sony M-O drive.

Sunstone, Inc.
POB 807
Plainsboro, NJ 08536
609.452.9523
Research, development, and manufacturer of rewritable optical media based on infrared phosphors.

SuperMac Technology
485 Potrero Avenue
Sunnyvale, CA 94086
408.245.2202
Based on Sony M-O drive, the firm offers the DataFrame RS Optical Drive.

Symmetrical Technologies, Inc. (Symtech)
301 Gallaher View Road, Suite 231
Knoxville, TN 37919

615.690.3838
Offers the M-OST rewritable optical subsystem for Sun workstations, Macintosh, and DEC VAX computers. M-OST is an acronym for magneto-optic storage technology and is based on the Sony M-O drive.

Tandy THOR-CD Technologies
1300 One Tandy Center
Fort Worth, TX 76102
817.390.3693
Announced rewritable compact optical disk media and drive system, THOR-CD (THOR stands for Tandy High-intensity Optical Recording), based on Optical Data, Inc.'s technology. Media to play on a standard CD audio player. In 1990 Tandy announced an indefinite delay beyond a 1991 target date for the introduction of THOR-CD. Development will focus on a consumer audio version of THOR.

TDK Electronics Corporation
12 Harbor Park Drive
Port Washington, NY 11050
516.625.0140

Teijin, Ltd.
Exploratory Research Laboratory
Tokyo Research Center
4-3-2, Asahigaoka Hino
Tokyo, 191 Japan
Purchased license of ODI's flexible rewritable optical media and is currently working on commercialization of the media.

Ten X Technology, Inc.
4807 Spicewood Springs Road
Building 3, Suite 3200
Austin, TX 78759
512.246.8360
Developed subsystem, Opti Xchange, based upon Pioneer's multifunction optical disk drive. Available for IBM RS/6000 (Reduced Instruction Set Computer-RISC)-based workstation and for PS/2 family of computers.

Toshiba America
9740 Irvine Blvd.
Irvine, CA 92718
714.583.3000

Tosoh USA, Inc.
800 C Gateway Blvd.
South San Francisco, CA 94080
415.588.5200

Trimarchi
P.O. Box 560
State College, PA 16804
814.234.5659
The Equalizer series offers Las-er-ase, a rewritable optical disk drive, to Microvax 2000 users. Configuration uses either Sony or Ricoh 5.25-inch M-O rewritable drives.

   The Datakeg Twin Sixes are optical disk drives for DEC, Sun, Macintosh, and IBM-PC users. Dual drives offer Winchester technology and provide rewritable optical storage as a backup.

U.S. Design Corporation
A Maxtor Company
4311 Forbes Blvd.
Lanham, MD 20706
301.577.2880
Expanded the firm's Q-Stor family of storage systems to include Sony rewritable optical drives for DEC and Sun platforms. Systems integrator for DEC and Sun computers. Software products include JukeVOX for the Sony jukebox.

University of Iowa
Weeg Computing Center
Lindquist Hall, Room 229
Iowa City, IA 52242
319.335.5470
Developed a WORM-based system for storing medical images for purposes of medical education. WORM and rewritable end-user.

University of Washington
Hospital Center
Seattle, WA
206.548.6725
Imaging application using Jasmine DirectOptical Macintosh-based subsystem.

Verbatim Corporation
Subsidiary of Eastman Kodak
1200 W. T., Harris Blvd.
Charlotte, NC 28213
704.547.6500
TMO 5.25-inch is available in both 512 and 1024 sector versions. Signed joint venture agreement with Mitsubishi to market Verbatim's 3.5-inch magneto-optic rewritable optical disks in Japan.

Verbatim's Optical Heads and Services Group provides optical head design, testing, and pilot manufacturing services.

Victory Enterprises
Victory Plaza
1011 East 53 1/2 Street
Austin, TX 78751-1728
800.421.0103
512.450.0801
Offers the OptiSAFE subsystem supporting Pioneer multifunction drive as well as Panasonic WORM and Maxoptix, Ricoh, and Sony rewritable disk drives.

Wangtek
41 Moreland Road
Simi Valley, CA 93065

Western Digital Corporation
2445 McCabe Way
Irvine, CA 92714
714.863.0102
WDATXT-FASST is an SCSI host bus adapter kit for the connection of WORM, rewritable, and CD-ROM drives and other peripherals to IBM-PC and compatible computers.

Workstations Solutions, Inc.
9 Trafalgar Square
Nashua, NH 03063
603.880.0080
Offers rewritable optical disk subsystem for Apollo (subsidiary of Hewlett-Packard) using Sony M-O drive; a maximum of seven subsystems can be connected to one workstation.

XYXIS Corporation
7084 Shady Oak Road
Eden Prairie, MN 55344
612.944.8288
Offers the Y600RW series of rewritable optical storage subsystems based on the Ricoh M-O drive for Sun, Macintosh, and IBM and compatible microcomputers.

Zetaco Corporation
6850 Shady Oak Road
Eden Prairie, MN 55344
612.941.9480
The Model SKR-600 is a rewritable optical subsystem compatible with Data General's MV series of minicomputers. It includes a Sony M-O 5.25-inch rewritable disk drive, a Data General-emulating disk controller, and an SCSI cable.

Appendix Two:

Recommended Readings

Alpert, M. "500,000 Pages on One Erasable Disk." *Fortune* (January 2, 1989).

Apiki, S., and H. Eglowstein "The Optical Option." *Byte Magazine* (October 1989): 160-174.

Araki, S., A. Asauama, and H. Kobayashi. "Magneto-Optical Writing System with the Pulse Magnetic Field." *IEEE Translation Journal on Magnetics in Japan* 691 (1985).

Asano, S. et al. "Magneto-Optical Recording Media With New Protective Films." In *IEEE Transactions on Magnetics* (1987): 2620-2622.

Balafas, D.M. "Attaching Removable-Media Drives Via the File System." *Systems Integration* (November 1989): 23-24.

Balma, P. "Impact of Erasable Optical Disks on Write-Once." In *Conference Proceedings of Optical Information Systems '88*, edited by Judith Paris Roth, 49-50. Westport, CT: Meckler Corporation, 1988.

Barton, R. et al. "New Phase-Change Material For Optical Recording With Short Erase Time." *Applied Physics* 48, no. 19 (1986): 1255-1257.

Bate, G. "Materials Challenges in Metallic, Reversible, Optical Recording Media: A Review." In *IEEE Transactions on Magnetics*, (1987): 151-161.

Bell, A. "Erasable Self-Biasing Thermal Magneto-Optic Medium." European Patent #86111465.0 (1986).

—— "Materials For High-Density Optical Data Storage." In *CRC Handbook of Laser Science and Technology, Volume I*, edited by M. Weber.Boca Raton, FL: CRC Press, 1986.

Berg, B.A. "Software Considerations for Multifunction and Rewritable Optical Storage." *Optical Information Systems* 10, no.6 (November/December 1990).

Berg, B.A., and J.P. Roth. *Software for Optical Storage*. Westport, CT: Meckler Corporation, 1989.

Berry, D. "How a Computer Media Manufacturer Approaches Erasable Optical Media Development." In *Conference Proceedings of Optical Information Systems '88*, edited by Judith Paris Roth, 42-43. Westport, CT: Meckler Corporation, 1988.

Birecki, H. et al. "Magneto-Optic Quadrilayer Reliability and Performance." In *Proceedings of the Society of Photo-Optical Instrumentation Engineers*, (1985): 19-24.

Bloomberg, D. and G. Connell. "Magnetooptical Recording." In *Magnetic Recording, Volume III.*, edited by C. Mee and E. Daniel. New York: McGraw-Hill, 1988.

Bouwhuis, G., J. Braat, A. Huijse, J. Pasman, G. Van Rosmalen, and K. Schouhamer-Immink. *Principles of Optical Disc Systems*. Accord, MA: Adam Hilger, Ltd., 1985.

Bradley, A.C. *Optical Storage for Computers: Technical and Applications*. Ellis Horwood Books in Information Technology. New York: John Wiley & Sons, 1989.

Burke, J.J., and B. Ryan "Gigabytes On-Line." *Byte Magazine* (October 1989): 259-264.

Canon USA, Inc. *Introduction to Magneto-Optic Technology: What Is Magneto-Optic Storage?* Lake Success, NY: Canon USA, Inc., 1989.

Connell, G.A.N. "Magneto-Optics and Amorphous Metals: An Optical Storage Revolution." *Journal of Magnetism and Magnetic Material* 54, no. 333 (1986): 1561-1566.

Cook, E.A. "Rewritable Disks at Work in Remote Sensing/GIS." *Advanced Imaging* (September 1989): 68, 71.

Costlow, T. "Erasables to Lead Op[tical] Drives Surge." *Electronic Engineering Times* (April 10, 1989).

Daly, J. "Erasable Optical Disks Step Closer to Forefront." *Computerworld* (April 10, 1989): 25, 34.

Furuhata, H., Y. Konno, H. Fueki, Y. Shikano, S. Okada, S. Niizawa, and R. Naito "Development of an ISO Sampled Servo Rewritable/Write-Once Combination Optical Disk Drive." *Japanese Journal of Applied Physics* 28 (1989): 77-80.

Gaskin, R.R. "Paper, Magnets, and Light." *BYTE Magazine* (November 1989): 391-399.

Gravesteijn, D.J. "Materials Developments for Write-Once and Erasable Phase-Change Optical Recording." *Applied Optics* 27, no. 4 (1988): 736-738.

Gunn, Keith. "File Structure Standards." *Optical Memory News* 63 (1988): 6-7.

Hamilton, W. "Pioneer Demonstrates First 5.25-inch Multifunction MO Drive." *Optical Memory News* 85 (July 1990): 1, 4.

Harvey, D.A. "Optical Storage Primer." *Byte* (Fall 1990): 121-130.

"H-P Developing 5.25-inch Multifunction Drive Using MO in Write-Once Mode." *Optical Memory News* (August 1990): 1, 14.

Hoy, J.J. *Write-Once or Not Really Write-Once (When is This a Question).* White Paper. Colorado Springs, CO: Laser Magnetic Storage International, 1990.

Introduction to Magneto-Optic Technology: What is Magneto-Optic Storage? Published by Canon USA, Inc. 1989.

Isailovic, J. *Videodisc and Optical Memory Systems.* Englewood

Cliffs, NJ: Prentice-Hall, Inc., 1985.

Kalstrom, D. *Compatibility Is the Key to Success for New Computer Technologies*. Plasmon Data Systems, Inc., 1988.

———"Hard Disk Vs. Erasable Optical Storage." *Computer Systems News* (May 1, 1989): 17.

———"Form Follows Multifunction." Letter to the Editor, *Computer Systems News* (August 27, 1990): 15.

Kume, M., K. Ito, and G. Kano "Semiconductor Lasers for WORM, Erasable and Rewritable Memory Disks." *Journal of Electronic Engineering* 24, no. 248 (1987): 44-47.

Kwok, C. "Implementing WORM and Erasable Optical Storage in the OS/2 Environment." In *Software for Optical Storage,* edited by B.A. Berg and J.P. Roth. Westport, CT: Meckler Corporation, 1989.

Lapedus, M. "H-P Sees Broad Market for Erasable Drive." *Electronic News* (April 17, 1989): 24.

McCready, S. "CD-WORM and Erasable Versus WORM: The Future Battle." In *Conference Proceedings of Optical Information Systems '88,* edited by Judith Paris Roth, 125-127. Westport, CT: Meckler Corporation, 1988.

Marchant, A.B. *Optical Recording: A Technical Overview*. Reading, MA: Addison-Wesley Publishing Company, 1990.

Meyer, F. "Erasable Optical: No Hard Disk Replacement." *Computer Technology Review* (May 1, 1989): 24.

———"Erasable Optical No Market Threat." *Computer Technology Review* (March 1989): 26.

Minemura, H., N. Tsuboi, and Y. Sato "Erasable Characteristics of Optical Disks Using Induction Heating." *Transactions of the Institute of Electronic Information Communication Engineers* 3 (1988): 486-91.

Nagato, K., A. Kawamoto, T. Sato, and Y. Yorozu. "Compositional Dependence of Recording Noise in Amorphous Rare-Earth—Transition-Metal Magneto-Optical Discs." *Journal of Applied Physics* 63 (1988): 3856.

"The NeXT Debut: The Computing Landscape Changes." *Seybold Report on Desktop Publishing.* Media, PA: Seybold Publications, Inc., October 12, 1988.

Primer on Multifunctional Optical Storage, A. San Diego, CA: Hewlett-Packard, 1990.

"Panasonic Introduces Phase-Change 5.25-inch Drive." *Optical Memory News* 85 (July 1990): 1, 6.

"Pioneer Multifunction Drive Uses Sampled Servo Format." *Optical Memory News* 85 (July 1990): 5.

Radoff, D. "New Choices in Storage." *Unix World* (April 1989): 69-72.

"Rewritable Optical Storage Enhances LANs." *LAN Times* (July 1,1989): 36.

Roth, J.P. *Rewritable Optical Storage Technology.* Westport, CT: Meckler Corporation, 1990.

Rothchild, E. "1990: The Year of the Rewritable Drive." *Optical Memory News* 79 (January 1990): 1, 9-13.

———*Rewritable Optical Media and Technology Markets.* San Francisco, CA: Rothchild Consultants, 1988.

Saffady, W. *Optical Storage Technology 1989: A State-of-the-Art Review.* Westport, CT: Meckler Corporation, 1989.

———*Micrographics and Optical Storage Equipment Review.* Volume 15. Westport, CT: Meckler Corporation, 1990.

Scholte, P.M.L.O., and D.J. Gravesteijn "New Materials for Reversible Optical Storage Applications." In *Video, Audio, and Data Recording — Proceedings of the Seventh International Conference.* London: IERE 79 (1988): 11-14.

Schroeder, C. "Information Standards and Optical Disk Systems." *Inform* 1, no. 2 (1987): 12-13.

Seiter, C. "Erasable Opticals: New Light on Data." *Macworld: The Macintosh Magazine* (March 1990): 152-159.

Shieh, J., and M. Kryder. "Magneto-optic Recording Materials with Direct Overwrite Capability." *Applied Physics Letters* 49 (1986): 473.

Soat, J. and W. McClatchy "A Different Orientation." *Information Week* (February 12, 1990): 46-47.

Tanaka, K., I. Watanbe, and H. Sugahara. "The Technical Trends in Optical Disk Storage." *Information Processing Society of Japan* 28, no. 8 (1987): 1075-1083.

"Ten X Subsystem Uses Pioneer 5.25-inch Multifunction Drive." *Optical Memory News* 85 (July 1990): 4.

Terdoslavich, W. "Optical Storage: Multifunction Grows." *Computer Systems News* (July 23, 1990): 35-36.

Tevanian, Avadis, Jr., and B. Smith "Mach: The Model for Future UNIX." *BYTE Magazine* (November 1989): 411-416.

Thomas, G.E. "Future Trends in Optical Recording." *Philips Technical Review* (Netherlands) 44, no. 2 (1988): 51-57.

Thompson, T. and Nick Baran. "The NeXT Computer." *Byte Magazine* 13, no. 12 (November 1988): 158-175.

Understanding Computers: Memory and Storage. Alexandria, VA: Time-Life Books, Inc., 1987.

Van Dyke, B. "SCSI: The I/O Standard Evolves." *Byte* (Fall 1990): 187-191.

Warren, C. "Software Tools, Utilities Drive Optical Disks." *Mini-Micro Systems* 19, no. 15 (December 1986): 33-44.

Webb, D. "Erasable Optical Comes of Age." *Computer Systems News* (June 5, 1989): 33.

Webster, B. *The NeXT Book.* New York, NY: Addison-Wesley, 1989.

———"What's NeXT?" *Macworld: The Macintosh Magazine* (January 1989).

Glossary

acceleration - The rate of change of speed with time. In optical storage, one measure of the severity of the job to be accomplished by the focus and tracking servos in correcting flatness.

access time - The time to get to a specified location in or on a memory device. For disk drives, quoted access times usually refer only to the positioning time for the radial actuator, neglecting servo settling and rotational latency; average access times for disk drives usually describe a radial motion of one-third of a full stroke. See **latency**.

access time - controller (read) - The time measured from the drive's receipt of a SEEK command (if necessary) from the controller to the time the first byte of data is received by the controller. Therefore, it includes seek time and latency, as well as the time to read and transfer the first byte of data.

access time - controller (write) - The time measured from the drive's receipt of a SEEK command (if necessary) from the controller to the time the first byte of data is written to the disk. Therefore, it may include seek time, head settling, latency, and writing the first byte.

access time - host (read) - The time measured from the controller's receipt of the last byte of a READ command block from the host to the time the first byte of data is available to the host.

For controllers that perform a simple read-ahead or some sophisticated caching algorithm, the READ command may not require any disk access since the necessary data is already available in the controller buffer. For these controllers, host read access time would only include command validation and DMA (or other data transfer) set-up time to send the first byte of data to the host.

For controllers that always require a disk access, host read access time consists of command validation, seek time, latency, reading, error detection and correction, and DMA (or other data transfer) set-up time to send the first byte of data to the host.

anode - Terminal, realized as a structure such as a wire, plate, or grid into which electrons flow.

ANSI (American National Standards Institute) - Organization that approves standards used by numerous industries in the United States.

ASC (Accredited Standards Committee) - Committee that works on projects intended to become ANSI standards.

attitude - Position of an optical disk cartridge that is determined by the relationship between its axes and a reference plane.

axial acceleration - The acceleration of the recording layer along the fixed line normal to the disk reference plane at a specific rotational frequency (speed), as sensed by the optical system.

axial deflection - The deflection of any point of the recording layer from its nominal position with respect to the disk reference plane as determined by the nominal optical thickness of the protective layer, in a direction normal to the reference plane.

B - Abbreviation for bytes. Used as a suffix, e.g., MB.

b - Abbreviation for bits. Used as a suffix, e.g., Kb.

backwards compatible - Sometimes "downward compatible"; said of a new product that can be used with equipment or media originally designed for use with an older product. An example is an erasable medium that can be written and read by a drive that was originally produced to read and write WORM media.

bad sector - An unusable portion of a disk caused by a media defect.

A bad sector table retains these locations and prevents their access.

BIOS (Basic Input/Output System) - A set of ROM-resident device drivers for an IBM-PC or compatible computer. Drivers are included for the keyboard, console, printer, floppy disk, and hard disk.

block - An amount of data moved or addressed as a single unit; the least amount of data to be read or written at a time. Deciding what size a block should be involves trade-offs. Error correction will use the least additional storage space when blocks are long, but storage space is wasted if a data file is smaller than a block. Typical block sizes in WORM drives are 512, 1024, 2048 bytes.

burst error - In error correction for a storage device, the loss of many consecutive bits of information because of some flaw in the medium such as a scratch or dirt. The distinction is with continuous noise which corrupts data in a different way, requiring a different kind of error correction. In optical memory, most data loss is due to burst errors. The design of an error correction code (ECC) depends on how often error bursts are likely to occur and how long the longest burst is likely to be.

burst mode - A method of transferring data that does not permit an interrupt to occur.

cache - Generally, temporary storage for data to which access must be very quick.

cartridge - An enclosure (generally of plastic) in which an optical medium (disk) is kept for protection. Some vendors captivate their media in the cartridge (this mode is called "spin in"), providing a window for the laser beam; others remove the medium from the cartridge inside the drive. Also called a cassette.

case - Housing for an optical disk that protects the disk from damage arising from handling. May also be used for labeling, write inhibit features, and media identification holes.

CAV (Constant Angular Velocity) - Describes the characteristic of a disk which always spins at the same rotational rate, so that the time it takes to scan a track is the same at all radii.

CCS (Common Command Set) - A set of standard SCSI commands and data structures defined in a document produced by a task group of the SCSI ASC (X3T9.2). Revision 4.B (23 June 1986) is the definition by which a device is termed "CCS-compliant," but it will be part of the SCSI-2 standard. The CCS allows a driver to dynamically determine the characteristics of devices attached to an SCSI port.

CCS (Continuous Composite Servo) - A physical format for optical media in which servo information is continuously encoded on the disk. It is one of three competing formats for standardizing 5.25-inch WORM media, and the only proposed 5.25-inch erasable optical format.

CCW (Continuous Composite Write-Once) - Combines basic principles of magneto-optical (M-O) recording with write-once (W-O) protection methods. CCW media is M-O media with factory stamped codes on control tracks to identify media as W-O. Factory stamped codes make the media incompatible with other rewritable optical disk drives. Additional overwrite protection is added at initialization and write (DDS field and blank checking).

CD-ROM (Compact Disc, Read-Only Memory) - A version of the standard compact disc intended to store general purpose digital data, although CD audio data can also be included. Its data capacity is upwards of 600MB.

CIRC (Cross-Interleaved Reed-Solomon Code) - Using a sophisticated method of error detection and correction (a layered error correction code) that involves techniques of data delay and data rearrangement techniques, corrected data can be one bit error in a trillion bits. CIRC detects and corrects up to two errors in one code word and interpolates for long error bursts. The maximum complete correctable error burst length is 4,000 data bits, and the maximum worst case interpolatable burst is 12,300 data bits assuming that no random errors occur at the same time.

clamping zone - Annular part of the disk within which the clamping force is applied by the clamping mechanism.

CLV (Constant Linear Velocity) - Describes the characteristic of a disk which rotates more slowly when outer radii are being scanned so that the relative velocity between a writable "cell" and the track is maintained at a constant value. This keeps the linear density of data constant over the whole disk, but creates practical problems due to the non-constant time taken to scan one track and the need to speed up and slow down the disk as various radii are scanned.

CNR (Carrier-to-Noise Ratio) - (1) the ratio of the root-mean-square (RMS) power of a signal at a specified frequency to the RMS power of the noise in a specified bandwidth, expressed in decibels (dB). (2) The ratio of the carrier level to the level of noise also found in the channel of interest. CNR has value mostly as an arbitrary figure with which most individuals are familiar.

coercivity - The strength of a magnetic field required to change the existing magnetic state of a material. Magnetic materials lose coercivity as the temperature rises.

collimator - A device such as a lens that turns an available light beam into a parallel (collimated) beam.

collimator pen - A specific commercial device containing a semiconductor laser and collimating optics. It is used in optical heads to provide a beam suitable to send to the focusing lens.

compensation tempature - The temperature at which the magnetization of a ferrimagnetic material goes to zero; also known as compensation point. M-O materials which are ferrimagnetic are often written by bringing them locally up to the compensation point in the presence of a weak, poorly localized magnetic field.

compression - An encoding technique that saves storage space by eliminating gaps, empty fields, redundancy, or unnecessary data, to shorten the length of records or blocks. Provides for the use of fewer data bits than originally required without information loss. A decoding technique implements the reverse operation to convert it to the original data.

concatenated code - System involving two successive codes, generally two (n,k) codes in which the two "n's" are relatively prime.

control track - Used for pre-recording media parameters and format information necessary for reading and writing the disk.

CRC (Cyclic Redundancy Check) - A simple form of algebraic error correcting code.

cross talk level - Ratio of the level of a spurious signal generated by an adjacent track to the level of the signal of that adjacent track.

crypto errors - Defects that cannot be detected by acceptance testing of a new incoming optical disk cartridge but only become apparent when writing is attempted.

Curie point recording - Writing, for example on an M-O disk, by bringing the temperature locally up to the Curie point so that a weak magnetic field can magnetize the heated spot.
     The Curie point is the temperature at which a magnetic matrial becomes easier to magnetize. The laser heats a spot on the magnetic film to 150°C (the M-O disk's Curie point), allowing the M-O drive's magnet to change the bit's magnetic polarity.

Curie temperature - The temperature above which a material loses any magnetization.

DASD (Direct Access Storage Devices) - IBM nomenclature for a storage peripheral that can respond directly to random requests for information.

defect - Some irregularity in a medium that disturbs its ability to store recorded data. Defects in an optical disk include bumps, depressions, dirt, missing sensitive material, etc. Because of the high density of optical recording, even micrometer-sized defects are of consequence.

defect density - The fraction of the total active area of a medium obscured by defects.

Digital Paper - A relatively new optical storage flexible media that has a storage capacity of one gigabyte on a single-sided 5.25-inch optical disk. BOSCO (Bernoulli Optical Systems Company), an offshoot of Iomega Corporation, is developing a 5.25-inch WORM drive that uses "floppy" WORM disks.

Developed by ICI Imagedata, part of ICI Films which is a business unit of ICI Americas, Inc., this "floppy" optical media is produced by sputtering a reflective layer onto a polyester film substrate and then coating the material with a dye polymer (D-P) layer. The dye can be tuned to suit the infrared wavelength of the writing laser. Data is encoded by the difference in reflectivity between the unburned material and the micropits formed by laser action. The data densities achievable are a function of the wavelength of the laser. Current technology can produce and resolve pits of one micrometer in diameter using solid state lasers with a wavelength of 780 to 830 nanometers. A data density of greater than 10MB per square inch is attainable.

disk reference plane - Defined by the flat annular surface on an ideal spindle which contacts the clamping zone of the disk and is normal to the axis of rotation.

DRAW (Direct-Read-After-Write) - Describes the method of error checking in which data written to an optical disk during one disk rotation is read for accuracy on the subsequent rotation. Recorded data on an optical disk may be read immediately after writing (recording); no processing is required.

DRDW (Direct-Read-During-Write) - Describes a method of error checking data on an optical disk in which data is written and verified during the same disk rotation. Refers to the ability to read the information during the writing process.

ECC (Error Correction Code) - A method of data recovery that allows the full recovery of a single physical block of user data. An encoding scheme turns a bitstream into a longer bitstream whose length comes from carefully designed redundancy. This is intended to enable the encoded bitstream to survive corruption by random noise and burst noise and still be decodable to the original bitstream without missing or incorrect data. Examples are CIRC and convolutional code.

ECMA (European Computer Manufacturers Association) - Standards body headquartered in Geneva, Switzerland whose functions in Europe are similar to those of ANSI in the United States.

EDC (Error Detection Code) - Used in conjunction with ECC to allow the detection of errors for correction.

erasable - Rewritable. See also **M-O (magneto-optic)**.

Faraday effect - Certain substances, when exposed to a magnetic field, will change the polarity of light passing through them. This polarity change is called the Faraday effect. Optical disks using the Faraday effect must be transmissive, rather than reflective.

FAT (Fat Allocation Table) - A table maintained by MS-DOS and OS/2 for the chain of sectors that comprise a disk file. Each logical disk typically contains a redundant pair of FATs.

ferrimagnetic - Weakly attracted by a magnetic field.

ferromagnetic - Strongly attracted by a magnetic field.

FIFO (First-In, First-Out) - A queue for storage of commands or data.

firmware - Software stored in read-only memory (ROM).

focus servo - Used in an optical disk drive to keep the reading and/or writing light spot focused on the information bearing surface, despite imperfections in the medium and drive mechanisms or externally imposed shock and vibration.

form factor - The size and shape of a product. For example, most 5.25-inch Winchester drives have the same dimensions so that they can fit interchangeably into computer cabinets. For the same reason, 5.25-inch optical drives have the same form factor as Winchesters.

GB - Gigabyte; 2^{30} bytes. The prefix "giga" means one billion.

handling zone - The part of a disk or cartridge that may be touched by a handling mechanism, e.g., in a jukebox.

heap - An array representation of a binary tree of data entities. Some WORM software products use a data heap to store a hierarchical file system in order to allow random file modifications in a manner that efficiently uses disk space on the W-O medium.

hub - Central feature on the optical disk which interacts with the disk drive spindle.

import/export slot - The slot used to add disks to or remove disks from a jukebox; also referred to as an exchange slot or mailbox.

inode - A data structure containing administrative information for a Unix disk file, e.g., name, type, size, and location of contents.

interleaving - The process of breaking up and reordering blocks of data to cause a long error burst to be turned, after de-interleaving, into many short bursts, each of which can be corrected by the error correction code (ECC) in use.

inventory - To compile a mapping table indicating the storage slot of each volume in a jukebox. This is done by reading a volume label from each disk surface in a jukebox.

IPC (Inter-Process Communication) - An operating system level scheme for message passing between programs.

IPI (Intelligent Peripheral Interface) - A standard for an interface between a CPU and a storage peripheral device. The IPI interface handles data rates up to 10 Mb/sec and is gaining support from several large companies including Eastman Kodak and IBM.

ISO (International Organization for Standardization) - Standards body formed after World War II to precipitate international standardization. Its functions are similar to ANSI and ECMA.

jukebox - An automatic media handler for optical disks and drives; also called a library. A jukebox may support multiple disks online with offline disks quickly accessed mechanically using a robotic arm. Jukeboxes are also used for magnetic tape drives.

KB - Kilobytes; 1024, or 2^{10} bytes.

Kb - Kilobits; 1024, or 2^{10} bits.

kB - 1000 bytes.

kb - 1000 bits.

Kerr effect - Certain substances, when exposed to a magnetic field, will rotate the plane of polarization of light reflected from them. This phase change is called the Kerr effect.

lands - The flat areas in between the pits on the surface of an optical disk.

latency - The component of the delay in access to data that comes from waiting for a disk to rotate to the desired azimuth. Average latency for a disk drive is usually calculated as one-half the rotational period.

LBA (Logical Block Address) - The number used to locate a particular block of data on a disk surface.

LDA (Laminated Disk Assembly) - An optical disk structure developed by Eastman Kodak for its 14-inch WORM media.

locality - A measure of the distance between commonly accessed files on a disk. Low locality refers to files placed at a distance from each other resulting in longer-than-average seek times during operation.

mapping - In a jukebox environment, the process of translating a volume name to a disk's slot number.

MB - Megabyte; 2^{20} bytes. The prefix "mega" means one million.

MCAV (Modified Constant Angular Velocity) - MCAV is a media format. In MCAV, the tracks are divided into bands or zones. Within any one band, the disk spins at a constant angular velocity and there is a fixed number of sectors per track. The relation between velocity and band location is similar to the velocity versus radius curve for CAV operation. MCAV allows greater data density than CAV, but without the performance compromise of CLV.

M-O (Magneto-Optic) - An optical storage technology which combines laser and magnetic methods to read and write from a platter. Information is written by local magnetization of a magnetic medium, using a focused light beam to produce local heating and consequent reduction of coercivity so that a moderately strong, poorly localized magnetic field can flip the state of a small region of high coercivity material. Reading is done either magnetically with inductive heads in close proximity to the medium, or optically through rotation of the plane of polarization of probing light via the Faraday effect or Kerr effect.

mount - (1) An operation that makes the contents of a volume available to a file system. (2) The act of determining the location of a volume in a jukebox and insuring it is spun up in a drive.

ms - Millisecond; 2^{-3} seconds. The prefix "milli" means one thousandth.

multifunction - Also referred to as hybrid.

OCR (Optical Character Recognition) - A process of recognizing characters or numbers in printed form through the use of photoelectric technology. Also called optical scanning.

optical head - An assembly within an optical drive containing the components that reflect laser light on the data surface of the disk and convert the reflected light into electrical signals that can be interpreted as data. Components in the optical head are the laser, lenses, prisms, a focusing mechanism, and a photodetector.

o.s. - Abbreviation for operating system.

OSI (Open Systems Interconnect) - A mass storage interface standard promulgated by the ISO.

positioning time - The time interval required to bring a transducer and the location of the required data on a data medium into the relative physical position necessary for the data to be read or written, e.g., the time required to position a head on a magnetic disk, i.e., seek time plus rotational delay minus some overlap.

QLV (Quantized Linear Velocity) - See **MCAV (Modified Constant Angular Velocity)**.

reference plane - A plane defined by the flat annular surface of an ideal spindle which contacts the clamping zone of the disk and which is normal to the axis of rotation.

rewritable - Erasable. See also **M-O (Magneto-Optic)**.

RFPI (Remote Front Panel Interface) - The remote electrical connection to the front panel controls of a disk drive. Used by a jukebox to spin up or down a disk in a drive.

SCSI (Small Computer System Interface) - A standard 8-bit parallel interface frequently used to connect computer peripherals to a computer. SCSI provides a logical rather than a physical command set in order to allow common commands to be used with a multitude of device types. Approved in 1986 as ANSI standard X3.131-1986 (also known as "SCSI-1"). SCSI-2 is currently in the standard review process.

sector - A triangular section of a disk surface within a track. A block of data is addressed by its track and sector numbers.

seek error - The drive's laser is unable to accurately locate user-requested data as a result of physical and/or mechanical problems such as vibration, disk surface irregularities, and poor laser focusing.

seek time - The time required to make a storage unit ready to access a specific location by selection or physical positioning. In optical disk technology, the time required to position the optical read/write head to the desired track.

It should be measured from the moment the drive receives a SEEK command from the controller to the time the controller is informed (and validates if necessary) that the desired track has been reached. For other than controller designers, seek time may be a mildly interesting piece of information but not a particularly useful one. Traditionally, disk drive manufacturers supply three average seek times: track-to-track, full-stroke, and one-third stroke.

serial access storage - A storage device in which the access time depends upon the location of the data on a reference to data previously accessed.

servomechanism - A combination of detector and actuator that continuously follows some variable quantity; examples are the focus and tracking servos of optical disk drives.

slot number - Numeric indicator of a location within a jukebox; could be a storage slot, optical drive or the mailbox (import/export slot).

spin-up - The time during which a drive accelerates a stationary disk to its operational speed.

spindle - Part of the drive that contacts the disk and/or hub.

superblock - A block on a Unix disk that describes the state of a file system, e.g., size and maximum number of possible files. It normally follows the boot block and precedes the inode list.

TB - Terabyte; 2^{40} bytes. The prefix "tera" means one trillion.

track - A circular path on which information may be stored on a disk surface. A track encompasses one rotation of the disk, and is divided into sectors.

tracking servo - The servo used in an optical drive to keep the reading and/or writing light spot centered on the information track, despite imperfections in the medium and drive mechanisms or externally imposed shock and vibration.

transfer rate - The rate at which data is transferred to or from a device, especially the reading or writing rate of a storage peripheral. Usually expressed in bits or bytes per second.

transfer rate - controller (burst) - The number of bytes transferred per second on the system bus between the host (or host adapter) and the controller buffer. The difference between the controller burst transfer rate and the drive user data transfer rate is one of the main factors used in determining how a group of controllers can concurrently transfer data on the system bus without any of their respective drives "hiccupping" (losing a rotation). As long as the controller buffer is getting rid of data faster than it is receiving it, a drive need not lose revolutions except for certain error-handling situations.

transfer rate - drive (absolute) - The average number of bytes transferred between the drive and the controller buffer per second. The rate includes all bytes transferred including ECC and CRC bytes. For controller designers this drive transfer rate is of interest; for end-users this is usually of little or no interest.

transfer rate - drive (user data) - The number of bytes of user data transferred between the drive and the controller buffer per second. It will be affected by the same characteristics given in the definition of the absolute drive transfer rate.

transfer rate - subsystem (read) - The number of bytes transferred to the host during execution of a READ command divided by the elapsed time in seconds from the controller's receipt of the last byte of the READ command until the (SCSI) command complete message is sent.

The variations in times due to the different controller algorithms enable controller vendors to legitimately be proud of the effective read transfer rate of subsystems which include their controller. A slower drive transfer rate can be masked by a caching algorithm so that the subsystem has an apparent instantaneous access time and its transfer rate approaches the controller burst transfer rate.

transfer rate - subsystem (write) - The number of bytes transferred from the host during execution of a WRITE command divided by the elapsed time in seconds from the controller's receipt of the last byte of the WRITE command block to the time that a completion status is available to the host.

The events required to execute a WRITE command differ among magnetic, WORM, and erasable optical drives. For erasable optical drives it may include SEEK time, latency, erasing all sectors to be written, reseeking to the first sector, and writing the data. Since WORM media cannot be certified by using a write operation, some drives require extra disk rotations to verify the data after it is written. Magnetic disks do not need the erasing or reseeking steps.

Some controllers provide completion status after the last data byte is received, but before the data is written to the media. This is sometimes advantageous time wise, but can be a problem if anything prevents successful writing subsequently.

unmount - (1) An operation that makes the contents of a volume unavailable to a file system. (2) The act of spinning down a drive, removing its disk, and placing it in a storage slot within a jukebox.

volume - (1) One unit of removable storage; the contents of one optical disk surface. (2) A "named" optical disk surface in a jukebox; its "name" (label) is usually stored in a prescribed location on its surface.

volume verification - The process of reading a volume label from a prescribed disk surface location and verifying it against what was expected.

WORM (Write-Once, Read-Many) - An optical technology that allows data to be written once and to be read back indefinitely.

write-inhibit feature - Physical interlock used to prevent overwrite on the optical disk.

ZCAV (Zoned Constant Angular Velocity) - See **MCAV (Modified Constant Angular Velocity)**.

Index

Contributors

Brian A. Berg, president of Berg Software Design, has been in the software industry since 1974, and has been a consultant since 1979. He has implemented device drivers and real-time software under Unix, MS-DOS, MTOS, VMS, and AOS. Since 1985, he has implemented a number of systems which use WORM and CD-ROM optical storage and the SCSI interface. His consulting activities have been with firms including Arix (Arete Systems) Corporation, Plexus Computers, Inc., TAB Products Company, Raytel Systems Corporation, E-mu Systems, Inc., TRW (Teknekron) Financial Systems, Acctex Information Systems (IMTECH), and Sequent Computer Systems. He is a contributing editor of *Document Image Automation* journal and an active participant in Optical Information System conferences in the United States and United Kingdom. He participates in and helps organize the IEEE Asilomar Microcomputer Workshop held annually near Monterey, California. He is editor of *Software for Optical Storage* with J.P. Roth (Meckler, 1989) and has published articles in *Systems Integration* and *Document Image Automation*. He has a B.S. in mathematics from Pacific Lutheran University and attended computer science graduate classes at Stanford University.

Kent F. Ekberg is director of marketing for Optical Memory Products at Pioneer Communications of America. He has also served as sales and marketing manager at a division of Grumman Corporation, responsible for optical disk-based imaging systems integration. At Sony Corporation of America, he held positions as a manager in corporate planning, business planning, and marketing related to new nonconsumer products, particularly computer and optical disk products. He has taught at Northeastern University, the City University of New York, and Stevens Institute of Technology. He has a B.A. with honors

131

from Hofstra University, an M.A. from New York University where he did doctoral work in English and American literature, and an Advanced Professional Certificate in strategic planning from the Stern Graduate School of Business at NYU. He was recently elected to the board of directors of the Optical Publishing Association, a trade group.

Anthony J. Jasionowski is the manager of MECA's Business Engineering Center, a new product and business development group with responsibility for several new consumer and industrial, data and video, optical and magnetic storage devices including CD-ROM, WORM, rewritable, multifunction optical and magnetic disk drives. He has been with Panasonic (Matsushita Electric Corporation of America - MECA) since 1971, holding various product planning positions related to consumer recording and storage devices including VCRs, cameras, camcorders and videodiscs.

Richard Miller is an applications engineer for Optical Memory Products for Pioneer Communications of America, where he provides engineering support for the company's CD-ROM, WORM, and rewritable products. He has a B.E.E. and an M.S.E.E. in laser and electro-optics from the Georgia-Pacific Institute of Technology where he did graduate research in image processing for machine vision systems.

Christine Roby is product marketing manager at Hewlett-Packard Company's Greeley Storage Division. She has worked for H-P for two years in product marketing and market research. Prior to joining H-P, she was employed by Electronic Data Systems and the Chevrolet Motor Division of General Motors. She has a bachelor's degree in industrial Engineering from General Motors Institute and an M.B.A. from the University of Michigan.

Judith Paris Roth has been involved with optical storage technology since 1979. She is editor-in-chief of *Document Image Automation* magazine and chairperson of Meckler Corporation's U.S.-based Document Image Automation Conference. She is editor of *Essential Guide to CD-ROM, CD-ROM Applications and Markets, Case Studies of Optical Storage Applications, Rewritable Optical Storage Technology,* and *Converting Infor-*

mation for WORM Optical Storage: A Case Study Approach. In addition, she is co-editor of *Software for Optical Storage* with Brian A. Berg. She has written extensively about optical storage technology in such publications as *Popular Computing, Journal of the American Society of Information Science, Association of American Publishers (AAP) Newsletter, Newsletter for Scholarly Publishing, High Technology,* and *Educational and Instructional Television.* She has worked on a variety of systems using optical storage including the design, development, and implementation of a CD-ROM financial currency exchange rate system, and a variety of videodisc-based systems including an electronic retail kiosk, basic skills education program for the military, and document storage and automation for the U.S. Department of Defense. She has an M.S.L.S. from Syracuse University and attended the Information Systems Seminar at the Sloan School of Management of the Massachusetts Institute of Technology in 1981.

Cris Simpson is an applications engineer in Pioneer's Atlanta, Georgia, office. He has a bachelor's degree in computer engineering from the Georgia Institute of Technology. Previously, he was with the Veterans Administration Rehabilitation Research and Development Center (Decatur, Georgia).

John J. Stevens is the product manager, Recordable Products, for Philips and Du Pont Optical Company (PDO). He is responsible for the product line management of all PDO recordable products including 5.25- and 12-inch WORM as well as 3.5- and 5.25-inch rewritable M-O media. Mr. Stevens joined PDO in 1986 as business development manager where he was responsible for strategic planning, competitive analysis, and new business development. Prior to PDO, he held numerous technical, marketing, and product management positions within the chemicals and plastics industry. He began his career at Union Carbide Corporation where he worked primarily with plastic material development for use within the electrical and electronics industries. He has a B.S. in chemical engineering from Northeastern University and an M.B.A. from Rutgers University.

Takeshi Yazawa is the general manager of Sony Corporation's Data Storage Laboratory for new R&D activity in Boulder, Colorado. He managed the project engineering for Sony's Rewritable Optical Disk